T. E. Perkins

Sabbath Carols

a new collection of music and hymns

T. E. Perkins

Sabbath Carols
a new collection of music and hymns

ISBN/EAN: 9783337089597

Printed in Europe, USA, Canada, Australia, Japan

Cover: Foto ©Lupo / pixelio.de

More available books at **www.hansebooks.com**

Sabbath Carols:

A NEW COLLECTION

OF

MUSIC AND HYMNS.

Prepared for the Use of Sabbath Schools

BY

THEODORE E. PERKINS,

AUTHOR OF

"THE SHINING STAR," "SUNDAY SCHOOL BANNER," "GOLDEN PROMISE," ETC.

NEW YORK:
Published by BROWN & PERKINS, 76 E. Ninth St.,
TWO DOORS FROM BROADWAY.
IVISON, PHINNEY, BLAKEMAN & CO., 47 & 49 Greene St.

[The Music and Words of this book being mostly original, permission for their use must be obtained from the author.]

Entered, according to Act of Congress, in the year 1868, by
THEODORE E. PERKINS,
In the Clerk's Office of the District Court of the United States for the Southern District of New York.

PREFACE.

IN the preparation of SABBATH CAROLS, the chief aim of the author has been to secure,

First, New Hymns of the best possible *Sabbath School* quality, pervaded with an evangelical spirit.

Second, To set these Hymns to melodies which should best express their spiritual sentiment, and at the same time be not only elevating in tone, but attractive to children and easy of performance.

Third, In addition to the above, a collection of old, familiar Hymns and Tunes has been inserted in the latter portion of *Sabbath Carols,* comprising the standard Sabbath School compositions of the age.

"Many a man, drifted into sin, has been brought to the foot of the cross by the remembrance of a Sunday-School song that buried itself like a rill beneath the layers of a worldly life, but burst forth again like a river through the crevice of a riven conscience."—REV. ROBERT LOWRY.

DEDICATED
TO THE
Sabbath-School Children of the United States,
BY
FANNY CROSBY.

Beautiful Sabbath Carols,
  Like the note of a silver bell,
Sweet are the songs ye bring us
  From a land where our loved ones dwell;
Carols for sunny childhood,
  And a season of riper years;
Carols for those that labor,
  And are sowing their seed in tears.

Songs of the new-born spirit
  Gleam forth on your snowy page
Songs for the lonely pilgrim,
  As he leans on the staff of age.
Sing of a home in glory,
  Oh, tell of the fields of rest,
Beautiful Sabbath Carols,
  Ye are heralds by angels blest.

Electrotyped by SMITH & McDOUGAL, 82 & 84 Beekman Street.

SABBATH CAROLS.

COME, LET US SING.

Words by Mrs. LYDIA C. BAXTER.   Music by T. E. PERKINS.

1. Come, let us learn to sing be-low, That we may sing in heaven; Earth's mel-o-dies, with gentle flow, Are sweet as breath of even. Sing on, sing on, till far a-bove, The an-gels join our songs of love; Sing on, sing on, till far above, The angels join our songs of love. Sing on, sing on, Sing on, sing on, sing on.

2. And when of Jesus' grace we sing,—Redemption's sweetest story, We seem to hear the sound of wings, And feel the heavenly glory. Sing on, &c.

3. The spirit mounts and soars away,
   Filled with ecstatic pleasure;
   As glory, like a cheering ray,
   Mingles with earthly measure.
   Sing on, &c.

4. And when on flow'ry hills of praise,
   The golden harps are given;
   Our glorious songs to Christ we'll raise,
   And fill the courts of heaven.
   Sing on, &c.

COME TO JESUS COME.

Words by FANNY CROSBY.　　　　　Music by JAS. M. NORTH.

1. Hark! the gentle spirit pleading, Come to Jesus, come;
Love and mercy interceding, Come to Jesus, come:
Kneeling at the mercy-seat, Lay your burden there;
He will pardon, he will save you, Come to Jesus, come.

2. Can you still neglect and grieve him?
　Come to Jesus, come;
Will you not with joy receive him?
　Come to Jesus, come;
Would you be forever blest,
　He will give you rest;
Be not faithless but believing,
　Come to Jesus, come.

3. Would you win a glorious treasure?
　Come to Jesus, come;
Would you find eternal pleasure?
　Come to Jesus, come;
Are you weak, on him rely,
　He is ever nigh;
Like a Shepherd he will lead you,
　Come to Jesus, come.

MARCHING ON TO GLORY.

Words by FANNY CROSBY.   *Music by* HENRY A. BROWN.

1 Gal-lant sol-diers, hear the trumpet sounding, Fill the ranks while ev-ery heart With ea-ger joy is bounding. We are marching, marching on to glo-ry, Ar-my of the Sunday school, We're bound to Canaan's land. See our ban-ner proud-ly wav-ing o'er us, While our Cap-tain cheers the way be-fore us.

D. S. for Chorus.

2.
Dear companions, we are glad to meet you;
Will you help our noble cause,
Oh join us, we entreat you,
Rally, rally round our standard waving,
Come and join our youthful van,
There's room enough for all,
Marching onward, all is bright before us,
Marching onward, swell the joyful chorus.

3.
We are young, but still the right pursuing,
We shall conquer by-and-bye,
Our cruel foes subduing,
Crowns are waiting, waiting for the faithful,
We shall wear them by-and-bye,
And shout the victory too.
We are going where the golden river,
Glides o'er Eden's sunny banks for ever.

WAITING BY THE RIVER.

2 There is darkness o'er the river,
    And its billows loudly roar,
    Yet the music of the angels
    Cheers us from the other shore.
        CHORUS. We are waiting, &c.

3 And the city, bright with glory,
    How its splendor charms the eye!
    Though we view it from a distance,
    We shall reach it by-and-bye.—CHORUS.

4 He has taken many a loved one,
    We have seen them leave our side,
    With our Saviour we shall meet them,
    When we cross the rolling tide.—CHORUS.

5 Through the lonely vale of shadows,
    When in triumph we have passed,
    In the happy land of promise,
    We shall meet our friends at last. CHORUS.

THE CONVERT'S SONG.

2. Lost and ruined, dark was my way;
   Mercy found me a wandering soul;
   And now like one of old I can say—
   Jesus has made me whole.—CHORUS.

3. Weeping mourner, trust in his word;
   Freely come, 'tis a Father's call;
   Oh, taste and see how good is the Lord!
   Come, there's room for all.—CHORUS.

PILGRIM, REST AWHILE.

Words by Miss FANNY CROSBY. W. H. PETTIBONE.

1. Lord, the way is cold and dreary, Scarce a beam of light I see; Let me plead thy gracious promise, Let me find repose in thee. Faint beneath my heavy burden, Cheer me with thy tender smile; I am weary, O my Father, Let the pilgrim rest a while.

2. Shield me till the night is over,
And the gathering storm is past,
Till the morning sun arising,
Fills my soul with joy at last.
Shining through my tears of sorrow,
Let me view thy loving smile;
Lead me to thy cross, my Father,
Let the pilgrim rest a while.

3. Thou canst turn my grief to gladness;
Thou canst make the desert bloom;
Thou canst light the gloomy portals
Of the dark and silent tomb.
May I rest with thee forever,
When the toils of life are o'er;
From the spring of joy eternal
May I drink, and thirst no more.

THE ANGEL BOATMAN.

Words by Mrs. LYDIA BAXTER. Music by T. E. PERKINS.

1. One by one we cross the riv-er, One by one we're ferried o'er;
2. One by one we come to Je-sus, As we heed his gen-tle voice;

One by one the crowns are giv-en On the bright, ce-les-tial shore.
One by one his vineyard en-ter, There to la-bor and re-joice.

Youth and childhood oft are pass-ing O'er the dark and roll-ing tide,....
One by one sweet flow'rs we gather In the glorious work of love,....

And the white-robed an-gel-boat-man Is the dy-ing Christian's guide;
Garlands for the an-gel-boat-man To con-vey to realms a-bove:

And the white-robed angel-boat-man, Bears them o'er the roll-ing tide.
And the white-robed angel-boat-man, Bears them to the realms of love.

3. One by one the heavy-laden
   Sink beneath the noontide sun;
   And the aged pilgrim welcomes
   Evening shadows as they come.
   One by one, with sins forgiven,
   May we stand upon the shore,
   Waiting till the angel-boatman
   Takes the helm, and guides us o'er;
   And the white-robed angel-boatman
   Lands us on the shining shore.

BLESSED REDEEMER.

Words by FANNY CROSBY. Music by JAS. M. NORTH.

2. Tranquilly fading, slowly declining,
Twilight is passing in beauty away;
Now on thy bosom safely reclining,
Teach us, our Father, oh, teach us to pray.
Blessed Redeemer, leave us, oh never,
Till we have anchored over the river,
Till we shall praise thee singing forever,
Jesus, our Saviour, glory to thee.

THE STONE ROLLED AWAY.

Words by Mrs. LYDIA BAXTER. Music by T. E. PERKINS.

3 Rejoicing in Jesus our union is sweet ;
As heirs of his kingdom each other we greet:
Together we love him, together we pray,
For angels of glory the stone rolled away.—CHORUS.

4 We'll sing of salvation through Jesus the Lamb,
'Till we on Mount Zion before him shall stand ;
Forever with Jesus, forever to stay,
For angels of glory the stone rolled away.—CHORUS.

HEAVEN OF REST.

Words by Rev. H. C. M'COOK.   Music arr. by JAS. M. NORTH.

1. While walking the vale, What shadows pre-vail, And how gloomy the clouds that ap-pear...... But in heaven, our home, Shall no shades ev-er come, No cloud nor no night shall be there.

Chorus.

O heaven, sweet heav-en, bright heav-en of rest; How hap-py we'll be, Dear Re-deem-er, with thee, Of its joys and its glo-ries pos-sessed!

2 What sorrow we know,
  What weeping and woe
In this valley of tears while we stay.
  But in heaven, our home,
  Shall no tears ever come,
For Jesus shall wipe them away.—Cho.

3 How weary we grow
  On our journey below,
As foot-sore and faint we press on.

But our toil shall be past
  In the heaven of rest,
Our weakness and weariness gone.—Cho.

4 No doubting, nor fear,
  Nor temptation is there,
Nevermore from our Shepherd we'll stray.
  But in glory above
  We shall live in the love
Of our Jesus for aye and for aye.—Cho.

14. ON OUR WAY TO GLORY.

2. Though afflictions darkly rise,
Veiling oft our native skies,
They are blessings in disguise,
   On the way to glory.
Let our hearts in God be strong,
Though our journey may be long,
Free salvation be our song
   On our way to glory.

3. Follow still our heavenly Guide,
Faithful in his love abide,
Laying every weight aside
   On the way to glory.
Grace will all our foes subdue,
Grace our vigor will renew,
Grace will bring us safely through
   Praise the Lord of glory.

FELLOW-HELPERS.

Words by Rev. E. TURNEY, D.D.   Music by A. VANALSTYNE.

2. Fellow-helpers to the truth,
    Lift your eyes, the fields are white:
Precious fruit o'er all the plain
    Doth the reaper's toil invite.
Enter now the harvest field,
    With united heart and hand:
Hark! a thousand urgent calls
    All your energies demand.

3. Fellow-helpers to the truth,
    Witness to its quickening power,
Till the sound of life and peace
    Echo back from every shore.
By the love of Christ constrained,
    Heaven's appointed work fulfill:
Here present your choicest gifts,
    Life, and wealth, and active zeal.

THE HAPPY LONG AGO.

Words by FANNY CROSBY. Music by T. E. PERKINS.

THE HAPPY LONG AGO. 17

2.
In the gentle summer breeze,
And the sign of closing day,
We have heard a tender carol
And the music seemed to say:
Weary pilgrims, journey on,
For the Saviour still is nigh;
He will bear you on his bosom,
You will meet us by-and-bye.
From the voices of the night
Comes a murmur soft and low,
From the parted ones that left us
In the happy long ago.
Cho. They are waiting, &c.

3.
They are waiting by the shore,
They will bid us welcome there,
"To the river clear as crystal,"
And the trees that bloom so fair.
With the angels we shall sing,
With our Saviour we shall dwell;
To the friends that warmly greet us
We shall never say farewell.
Kindred spirits, ever blest,
Where no tears of sorrow flow,
They will love as when we parted
In the happy long ago.
Cho. They are waiting, &c.

JESUS LOVES ME.
T. E. PERKINS.

1. Je - sus loves me, this I know, For the Bi - ble tells me so;
2. Je - sus loves me, loves me still, Tho' I'm oft - en weak and ill;

Lit - tle ones to him be - long—They are weak, but he is strong.
From his shin - ing throne on high Comes to watch me, where I lie.

Je - sus loves me, he who died Heav-en's gates to op - en wide;
Je - sus loves me, he will stay Close be-side me all the way,

He will wash a - way my sin, Let his lit - tle child come in.
Then his lit - tle child will take Up to heaven for his dear sake.

JESUS ONLY.

Arranged by JAMES M. NORTH.

3. Jesus rose, Jesus rose,
    Left the gloomy grave for me;
  Gained the victory o'er my foes,
    Conquered the last enemy;
  Peaceful I shall sleep in death
    Till his call shall set me free.
  Jesus rose, Jesus rose,
    Rose and left the grave for me.

4. Jesus lives, Jesus lives,
    Ever lives to plead for me—
  Day by day my sin forgives,
    Grants me grace his child to be;
  When immortal life he gives,
    I shall rise his face to see:
  Jesus lives, Jesus lives,
    Lives to intercede for me.

GRACE IS FREE.

2. Helpless at the cross I lay,
All my hope had well nigh fled,
Jesus took my sins away,
Jesus raised my drooping head.
Cho. Glory, &c.

3. Then I heard a voice divine
Gently bid me look and live;
Oh, what rapture now is mine!
Joy the world can never give.
Cho. Glory, &c.

4. Saviour, with my latest breath
Pard'ning grace my theme shall be,
Till I cross the waves of death,
Till I anchor safe with thee.
Cho. Glory, &c.

SABBATH BELLS.

Words by FANNY CROSBY.   Music by T. E. PERKINS.

1. Ring-ing, sweetly ring-ing, The cheerful Sabbath bells, Ringing, sweetly ring-ing, The cheerful Sab-bath bells. We lin - ger a mo-ment their call to hear, Then haste a - way to our school so dear, O - ver the greenwood joy - ous and free, Sing-ing with glad-ness, hap-py are we. *Chorus.* While o - ver the dis - tant hill Their mu - sic is float-ing still, Hear the ech - o, ech - o, ech - o,

SABBATH BELLS.

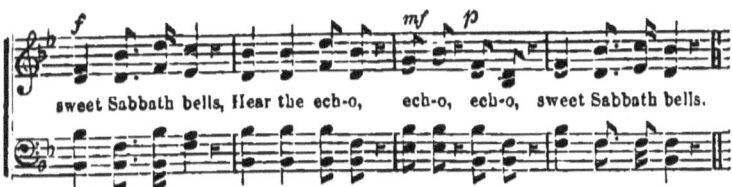

sweet Sabbath bells, Hear the ech-o, ech-o, ech-o, sweet Sabbath bells.

|: 2 Ringing, sweetly ringing,
  Their silver chimes we love, :|
A mission of peace to the heart they bear,
A welcome call to the house of prayer,
Telling of rapture, telling of rest,
Mansion of glory, tranquil and blest.
  CHO. While over, &c.

|: 3 Ringing, sweetly ringing,
  Those cheerful Sabbath bells. :|
O, let us be grateful to God above, [love,
Who crowneth our days with the light of
Blessed Redeemer, ever to thee
Praise from thy children offered shall be.
  CHO. While over, &c.

JESUS IS MINE.

Words by BONAR.   Music by T. E. PERKINS.

1. Fade, fade each earth-ly joy, Je-sus is mine! Break ev-ery ten-der tie, Je-sus is mine! Dark is the wil-derness, Earth has no rest-ing place, Je-sus a-lone can bless, Je-sus is mine!

Tempt not my soul away,
  Jesus is mine!
Here would I ever stay,
  Jesus is mine!
Perishing things of clay,
Born but for one brief day,
Pass from my heart away,
  Jesus is mine!

3 Farewell, ye dreams of night,
  Jesus is mine!
Lost in this dawning light,
  Jesus is mine!

All that my soul has tried,
Left but a dismal void,
Jesus has satisfied,
  Jesus is mine!

4 Farewell, mortality,
  Jesus is mine!
Welcome, eternity,
  Jesus is mine!
Welcome, O loved and blest,
Welcome, sweet scenes of rest,
Welcome, my Saviour's breast,
  Jesus is mine!

JOY AMONG THE ANGELS.

T. E. P.

1. There is joy among the angels, That fill the courts above,
Cho. There is joy, &c.
O'er a wand'ring soul returning To ask a Father's love.
When the heart is bowed beneath the cross, And tears repentant fall,
And the earnest prayer of faith can say, "Here, Lord, I give thee all."

2. There is joy among the angels,
   They tune their harps in Heaven,
When the new-born soul, with rapture
   Can feel its sins forgiven;
And the healing stream of pardoning grace
   Has washed its guilt away,
And the eye looks up without a cloud,
   And hails the opening day.—Cho.

3. There is joy among the angels,
   The shining portals ring,
When a band of happy children
   Their hearts to Jesus bring;
Like the tender breath of early flowers
   Their grateful songs shall rise,
Till the answering note from cherub choirs
   In Eden's vale replies.—Cho.

I WANT TO THINK OF JESUS.

Words by Rev. SAMUEL A. RHEA.

1. I want to think of Jesus 'Mid all my anxious care;
D. C. I want to talk with Jesus, And tell him all I feel,
I want to lean on Jesus, For he my burden bears;
For well I know my Jesus Will then his love reveal.
I want to walk with Jesus, Close to his loving side,
And see the wounds of Jesus, And know for me he died.

2.
I want look at Jesus
  By faith within the vail,
And draw my strength from Jesus,
  Whose word can never fail;
I want to ask of Jesus
  To keep me pure within,
And hear the voice of Jesus
  That pardons all my sins;
I want to sing of Jesus,
  Of all the sweetest name,
The dying love of Jesus
  To all around proclaim.

3.
I want to put on Jesus,
  And hide myself in him,
For 'neath the robe of Jesus
  I've no more guilt or sin;
I want to live with Jesus
  The endless life of love,
When safe at home with Jesus
  In paradise above;
I want to praise my Jesus
  On harp of burnished gold,
And shout the love of Jesus
  Through ages yet untold.

24. CHEERFULLY GIVE.

Words by FANNY CROSBY. Music by T. E. PERKINS.

1. Give! Give! cheer-ful-ly give, As God has given to thee; Do good to all, is the great command, And thine a crown shall be.... Give to the wid-ow and or-phan one, Whose bur-den is hard to bear.... Go, vis-it the homes that are poor and dark, And scat-ter thy treas-ures there.

2.
Give! give! cheerfully give!
Though small may be thy store,
Oh! not in vain was the widow's mite,
Then give, and trust for more.
Give to the weary, the sick and faint,
Oh, banish the tears they shed ;
But do it in meekness and love to Him
Who giveth thy daily bread.
Cho. Give! give! cheerfully give.

3.
Give! give! prayerfully give
Where'er thou canst relieve ;
And thou shalt prove it is far more blest
To give than to receive.
Give to the spread of the Gospel light,
To those by the Cross who stand ;
Wherever their mission, at home or abroad,
Oh, give with a bounteous hand.—Cho.

WE'LL WAIT TILL JESUS COMES.

Dr. MILLER.

1. O land of rest, for thee I sigh, When will the moment come,
When I shall lay my ar-mor by, And dwell in peace at home?

2. No tranquil joys on earth I know, No peaceful sheltering dome,
This world's a wil-der-ness of woe, This world is not my home.

CHORUS.

We'll wait till Je-sus comes, We'll wait till Je sus comes,
We'll wait till Je-sus comes, We'll wait till Jesus comes,
We'll wait till Je-sus comes, And we'll be gather'd home.

3. To Jesus Christ I fled for rest;
   He bade me cease to roam,
   And lean for succor on his breast,
   And he'd conduct me home.

4. I sought at once my Saviour's side,
   No more my steps shall roam;
   With him I'll brave death's chilling tide,
   And reach my heavenly home.

I'LL SING WITH ANGELS.

Words by Mrs. LYDIA BAXTER.   T. E. P.

1. Oh, could I with the an-gels sing, With pure and sin-less voice, I'll fly a-broad on tire-less wing, And bid the world re-joice;
I'd sing of Je-sus' pre-cious love, To cheer the ach-ing heart; And of that glo-rious rest a-bove, Where tears can nev-er start.

2. I'd sing how God so free-ly gave His on-ly Son to die; That sin-ners he from death might save, And raise them to the sky;
O won-drous love! sur-pass-ing thought! For me those mansions fair Were by the bless-ed Sav-iour bought, With price beyond com-pare.

Chorus.
Oh, there, be-neath that love-lit sky, I'll sing with an-gels by-and-bye;
Oh, there, be-neath that love-lit sky, I'll sing with an-gels by-and-bye.

3 Oh come, celestial Spirit, come
On wings of holy light;
And bear me to your glorious home,
Where all is pure and bright.
There shall I join the angel throng,
And soar on tireless wing,
And sing the everlasting song
Of glory to our King.—Cho.

THE PILGRIM'S JOURNEY.

Words by FANNY CROSBY. Music by W. H. DOANE.

2. Thou wilt never, never leave me,
   If I give myself to thee,
   Teach, oh, teach me how to praise thee,
   Tell me what my life should be.
   I would go, &c.

3. May thy ever gracious Spirit,
   Lead me in the way of truth,
   May I learn the voice of wisdom
   In the early days of youth.
   I would go, &c.

4. Oh, how sweet to rest confiding
   On thy word that can not fail,
   Strong in thee, whate'er my trials,
   Through thy grace I must prevail.
   I would go, &c.

28. BEHOLD THE LAMB OF GOD.

JAS. M. NORTH.

Behold the Lamb of God That takes our guilt away, The bright and morning star, that leads To ev-er-last-ing day: Behold the Lamb of God, The pure and holy one, Who in the gar-den wept, and said, Thy will, not mine, be done.

2. They nailed him to the cross—
He suffered, bled, and died,
And, with his last expiring breath,
'Tis finished, Lord, he cried.
Behold the Lamb of God!
The Mighty now to save,
Who rent the cruel bars of death,
And trampled o'er the grave.

3. O sinner, why delay—
Why still the Spirit grieve!
Give God your heart, he bids you come,
His promised grace receive.
Behold the Lamb of God!
The pure and holy one,
In meek submission learn to say,
Thy will, not mine, be done.

HOSANNA TO HIS NAME.

2. Now Christ is sitting far above,
   Yet bows his listening ear;
   And every child may seek his love,
   And feel his presence near:
   If not the pressure of his hand,
   By faith we may attain
   A glimpse of him, the blessed Lamb,
   Hosanna to his name.—Cho.

3. When Christ his loved ones shall embrace
   Upon the golden shore,
   We all shall see his glorious face,
   And praise him evermore:
   Judea's children there we'll meet,
   With hearts and souls aflame,
   And sing with them that song so sweet,
   Hosanna to his name.—Cho.

IF I COME TO JESUS.

W. H. DOANE. By permission.

1. If I come to Je-sus, He will make me glad; He will give me pleasure, When my heart is sad. If I come to Je-sus,
2. If I come to Je-sus, He will hear my prayer; He will love me dearly, He my sins did bear. If I come, etc.

Hap-py I should be, He is gen-tly call-ing Lit-tle ones like me.

3. If I come to Jesus
   He will take my hand,
   He will kindly lead me
   To a better land.
   If I come, etc.

4. There with happy children.
   Robed in snowy white,
   I shall see my Saviour
   In that world so bright.
   If I come, etc.

32. SOLDIER OF THE CROSS.

Words by Rev. H. C. COOK. Music by JAS. M. NORTH.

2 I'm a soldier, soldier of the cross,
Little soldier of the cross,
In the army of the Lord;
And the flag that floats above,
Is the banner of his love,
For my captain is the Saviour gone before
me.—CHORUS.

3 I'm a soldier, soldier of the cross,
Little soldier of the cross,
And I'm fighting for the crown.
Fierce enough will be the fray,
But I'm sure to gain the day,
For my captain is the Saviour gone before
me.—CHORUS.

SOLDIER OF THE CROSS. 33

4 I'm a soldier, soldier of the cross,
Little soldier of the cross,
And I know I'll win the crown.
With my armor always bright
I can put my foes to flight,
For my captain is the Saviour gone before me.—CHORUS.

5 I'm a soldier, soldier of the cross,
Little soldier of the cross
Marching where the captain leads.
Soon the battle will be o'er
We shall meet to part no more
On the verdant plains, the verdant plains of glory.—CHORUS.

A STARLESS CROWN.

Words by Mrs. LYDIA BAXTER.   Music by T. E. PERKINS.

With energy.

1. Oh, shall I wear a star-less crown In yon-der world of glo-ry?
   The wondrous sto-ry of the cross, The sufferings of the Sav-iour,
   Or will some lit-tle friend be found To whom I've told the sto-ry—
   Who died that he from world-ly dross Might win us to his fa-vor.

Full Chorus.

O hap-py day! O hap-py place! We soon shall meet to-geth-er,
Where Je-sus stands with smil-ing face To crown us his for-ev-er.

2 A youthful army now we stand
Our Captain's word is given,
We'll onward move, his blest command
Will guide us on to heaven.
When serried hosts shall gather round
The Lamb on Zion's mountain,
Oh, there may we in ranks be found,
Beside that healing fountain.
CHO.—O happy day, &c.

3 In kindness now we ask you all
To join our noble army,
Though sorrow here may sometimes fall,
And skies look dark and stormy.
Beyond the dark, beyond the gloom
A day of light is gleaming;
And glory, brighter than the sun,
On every face is beaming
CHO.—O happy day, &c.

I'LL SING OF JESUS.

P. P. VAN ARSDALE. By permission.

1. I'll sing of Jesus crucified, The Lamb of God who bled and died; A healing balm, a crimson tide, Flowed from his head, his feet, his side.

Chorus.
Above the rest this note shall swell, My Jesus hath done all things well, My Jesus hath done all things well.

2.
He sought me in the wilderness,
And found me there in deep distress;
He changed and washed this heart of mine,
And filled me with his love divine.
 Above the rest, &c.

3.
For what the Lord hath done for me,
For boundless grace so rich and free,
For all his mercies that are past,
I'll praise him while my life shall last.
 Above the rest, &c.

4.
When sorrow's waves around me roll,
His promises my mind console;
When earth and hell my soul assail,
His grace and mercy never fail.
 Above the rest, &c.

5.
When death shall steal upon my frame,
To damp and quench the vital flame,
I'll turn me to my Saviour's breast,
And there recline and sweetly rest.
 Above the rest, &c.

6.
And when we join the ransomed throng,
To chant the sweet immortal song—
With tuneful heart and voice and tongue,
We'll roll the lofty note along.
 Above the rest, &c.

7.
To him who washed us in his blood,
And made us kings and priests to God;
Hosanna we will ever sing,
And make the heavenly arches ring.
 Above the rest, &c.

ALWAYS WITH US. 35

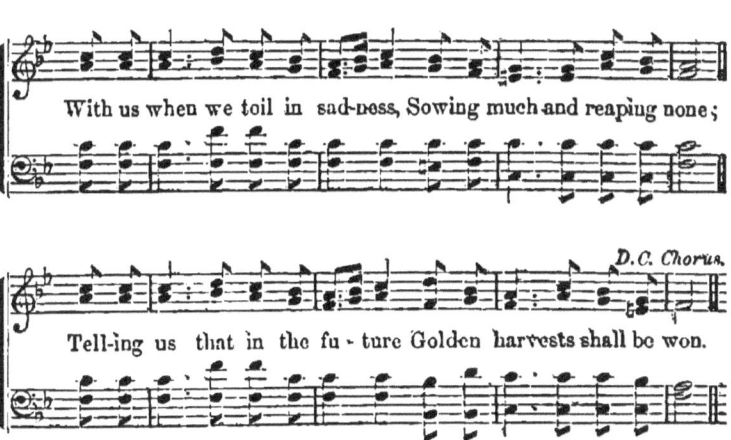

2. With us when the storm is sweeping
    O'er our pathway dark and drear;
Waking hope within our bosom,
    Stilling every anxious fear.
With us in the lonely valley,
    When we cross the chilly stream:
Lighting up the steps to glory,
    With salvation's radiant beam.
Always with us, always with us—
    Words of cheer and words of love,
Thus the risen Saviour whispers
    From his dwelling-place above.

SHALL I BE THERE.

Words by Mrs. LYDIA BAXTER. Music by T. E. PERKINS.

2 When teachers and scholars each other shall greet,
And join in the anthem at Jesus' dear feet,
Rich tokens of mercy for ever to share,
O tell me, dear Saviour, if I shall be there?
Chorus.—O tell me, &c.

3 When those, who have labored and struggled to save
Their loved ones from sorrow beyond the dark grave,
Are bringing the treasures they gathered with care,
O tell me, dear Saviour, if I shall be there?—Cho.

4 When life's dreary billows are spent on the shore
Beyond the dark river, and time is no more,
When bright palms of glory the victors shall bear,
O tell me, dear Saviour, if I shall be there?—Cho.

5 O blessed Redeemer, thy mercy and grace
Alone can prepare me to enter that place;
I'm stained and polluted, but shall I despair,
O tell me, dear Saviour, if I shall be there?—Cho.

"MORE LIKE JESUS."

Words by FANNIE CROSBY. Music by W. H. DOANE.
SLOW, WITH FEELING. *Written expressly for "Howard Mission."*

1. More like Je-sus would I be, Let my Sav-iour dwell with me; Fill my soul with peace and love— Make me gen-tle as a dove; More like Je-sus, while I go, Pil-grim in this world be-low,

D. C. Poor in spir-it would I be, Let my Sav-iour dwell in me;

2.
If he hears the raven's cry,
If his ever watchful eye
Marks the sparrows when they fall,
Surely he will hear my call.
He will teach me how to livn,
All my simple thoughts forgive;
Pure in heart I still would be—
Let my Saviour dwell in me.

3.
More like Jesus when I pray,
More like Jesus day by day,
May I rest me by his side,
Where the tranquil waters glide.
Born of him through grace renewed,
By his love my will subdued,
Rich in faith I still would be—
Let my Saviour dwell in me

38. LOOKING UNTO JESUS.

Words by FANNY CROSBY. Music by T. E. PERKINS.

1. Wea-ry not, my bro-ther, Cheer-ful be thy song; Is thy bur-den heav-y, And the jour-ney long? Does the weight op-press thee? Cast it on the Lord; Run thy race with pa-tience, Trusting in his word.

2. Seek and thou shalt find him, Still in faith be-lieve, Call and he will hear thee, Ask him, and re-ceive: In the dark-est mo-ment— In the deep-est night, He will give thee com-fort, He will give thee light.

Chorus.
Looking un-to Je-sus, He has died for thee, Oh, glo-ry be to Je-sus, We'll shout sal-va-tion free.

3. Trials may befall thee,
Thorns beset thy way,
Never mind them, brother,
Only watch and pray:
Through the vale of sorrow
Once the Saviour trod;
Run thy race with patience,
Pressing on to God.

4. Labor on, my brother,
Thou shall reap at last
Fruits of Joy eternal,
When thy work is past;
Crowds of shining angels
View thee from the skies,
Run thy race with patience,
Yonder is the prize.

WELCOME HOME.

Rev. R. LOWRY.

Duet. Cheerful.

1. There is a realm where Jesus reigns, A home of grace and love,
Where angels wait with sweetest strains To greet the saints above.

Chorus.

They'll sing their welcome home to me, They'll sing their welcome home to me; The Angels will stand on the heavenly strand, And sing their welcome home! Welcome home! Welcome home! The

2. There sons of earth will join to bless
   The precious Saviour's name,
   Clothed in his perfect righteousness,
   And saved from sin and shame.
       They'll sing their welcome, etc.

3. Yet all, alas! will not be there,
   For some will slight his grace,
   Though now he calls, they do not care
   To turn and seek his face.
       They'll sing their welcome, etc.

4. He speaks so kindly, "Come to me,
   And I will give you rest;"
   The angels wait their melody,
   To greet you with the blest.
       They'll sing their welcome, etc.

THE INVITATION.

2.
Where the temple stood in grandeur,
  Meekly riding, Jesus came,
By a countless throng attended,
  Shouting glory to his name.
Children then in love before him,
  Cried Hosanna in the throng;
Will you not like them adore him,
  Like them join the heavenly song?

CHORUS—CHILDREN.

Heavenly song! our happy voices
  Gladly join the sweet refrain;
Jesus came, and earth rejoices
  In the blessed Saviour's name.

3.
"Jesus died on Calvary's mountain;"
  Died to ransom you and me.
Will you not approach this fountain?
  Here salvation's full and free.
But our blessed Lord is risen:
  And he sits, a glorious King,
In the radiant light of heaven,
  Where adoring angels sing.

CHORUS—CHILDREN.

Angels sing: our youthful voices
  Gladly join the sweet refrain;
Jesus lives, and heaven rejoices;
  Hallelujah to his name.

NOTHING BUT LEAVES.

S. J. VAIL.

1. Nothing but leaves, the Spir-it grieves Over a wast-ed life; O'er sins indulged while conscience slept, O'er vows and prom-is-es unkept, And reap from years of strife— Nothing but leaves, Nothing but leaves.
2. Nothing but leaves, no gathered sheaves Of life's fair ripening grain; We sow our seeds, lo! tares and weeds, Words, i-dle words, for ear-nest deeds, We reap with toil and pain— Nothing but leaves, Nothing but leaves.

3.
Nothing but leaves, sad memory weaves;
  No vail to hide the past;
And as we trace our weary way,
Counting each lost and misspent day,
  Sadly we find at last—
    Nothing but leaves.

4.
Ah! who shall thus the Master meet,
  Bearing but withered leaves?
Ah! who shall at the Saviour's feet,
Before the awful judgment-seat,
  Lay down, for golden sheaves,
    Nothing but leaves?

HEAVEN IS BRIGHT.

Words by Mrs. LYDIA C. BAXTER. Music by T. E. PERKINS.

2. I know the songs of heaven are sweet,
   For one harmonious story
Of love and grace divinely meet,
   To swell the theme of glory.
Yes, heaven is bright, for God is light,
   Each ray his glory swelling;
And angels sing on tireless wing,
   The love of Jesus telling.

3. I've tasted here of Canaan's love,
   And joined in earth's hosanna,
But with the angels far above,
   I'll feast on heavenly manna,
Yes, heaven is bright, for God is light,
   Each ray his glory swelling;
And angels sing on tireless wing,
   The love of Jesus telling.

NEVER GIVE UP.

Words by Miss FANNY CROSBY. W. H. DOANE.

1. Soldiers for Jesus, remember our duty, He is our leader, and strong to defend; Gird on our armor and face every danger, Pray without ceasing and fight to the end. Never give up, never give up, never give up, never give up, But onward, march onward and never give up; never give up.

2. Never give up when the conflict is raging,
Sin is our foe, and the world is the field;
Stand by the cross with our banner uplifted,
Glory our watchword, the Bible our shield.—Cho.

3. Never give up when the night is the darkest,
Why should we tremble, there's nothing to fear;
Grace will support us, the Saviour still whispers,
Lo! I am with you, then be of good cheer.—Cho.

4. Cling to the hope that is sure as an anchor;
Trials, though often they mingle our cup,
Leave to the faithful a blessing behind them,
Bear them with patience, but never give up.—Cho.

5. Never give up till the foe we have conquered;
Firm at our post till our duty is done,
Stand we like heroes, and face every danger:
Never give up till the battle is won.—Cho.

THE BIBLE.

Rev. R. LOWRY. By permission.

3. What tells me where I soon must die,
And to the throne of judgment fly,
To meet the great Jehovah's eye?
It is the precious Bible.—Cho

4. Oh, may this treasure ever be
The best of all on earth to me,
And still new beauties may I see
In this the precious Bible.—Cho.

SPEAK, AND WE WILL HEAR.

1. Speak from thy ho- ly word, Bless thy waiting children here; Now in thy temple, Lord, oh speak, and we will hear. Ten- der- ly, watchful-ly guide our way, Chil-dren of thy fold are we,— Gently chide us when we stray, And bring us at last to thee.

2. Look from the mercy-seat,
   Where the shining angel throng
   Fall at thy sacred feet,
   And praise thee in their song.
    Cho. Tenderly, watchfully, &c.

3. God of eternal love,
   From thy temple ne'er depart;
   Come, thou celestial Dove,
   Abide in every heart.
    Cho. Tenderly, watchfully, &c.

46. OUR JESUS.

Words by Rev. T. A. T. HANNA. Music by W. F. SHERWIN.

1. Little birds of the forest, sweet, sweet be your song; Little brooks of the mountains, leap gladly along; Little flow'rs of the valley, ope wide your blue eyes, For our Jesus, dear Jesus, comes down from the skies. For our Jesus, dear Jesus, For our Jesus, dear Jesus, For our Jesus, dear Jesus, comes down from the skies.

2. Oh, the darkness that spread o'er Judea's blue sky,
And the rocks that were cleft at the finishing cry;
And the vail of the temple, all rending in twain,
When our Jesus, dear Jesus, for sinners was slain.
   When our Jesus, &c.

3. Hear the cry of the sea, as it breaks on the strand;
Hear the moan of the wind, as it sweeps o'er the land;
And the cedars of Lebanon mournfully wave—
For our Jesus, dear Jesus, goes down to the grave.
   For our Jesus, &c.

OUR JESUS.

4. But the armies of heaven triumphantly sing,
And the ramparts of Zion with clarions ring;
And each gate everlasting is lifting its head,
As our Jesus, dear Jesus, returns from the dead!
    As our Jesus, &c.

5. Oh, to stand with our foreheads illumed by his name,
And to thrill with the song of the slain, risen Lamb.
Oh, to wear the white robes, and the fresh palms to wave
To our Jesus, dear Jesus, the Mighty, to save.
    To our Jesus, &c.

CALL TO THE YOUNG.

P. P. VAN ARSDALE. By Permission.

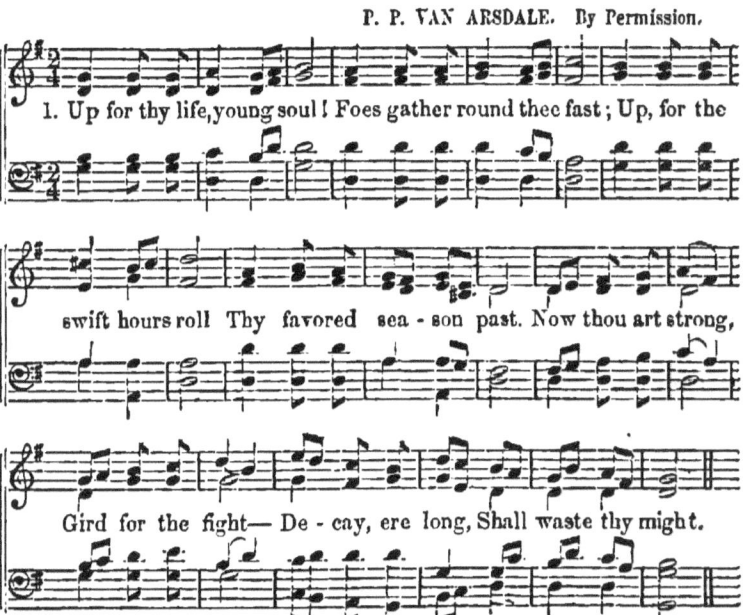

1. Up for thy life, young soul! Foes gather round thee fast; Up, for the swift hours roll Thy favored sea-son past. Now thou art strong, Gird for the fight— De-cay, ere long, Shall waste thy might.

2. Christ and his ransomed band
Toward heaven thy soul allure,
Glorious at his right hand,
While joys on high endure.
    There rest complete—
    Thrice welcome they,
    Whose early feet
    His call obey.

3. Mark now, from realms above
The Spirit o'er thee bends;
Gift of the Saviour's love,
Him, God the Father sends;
    He leads secure—
    His sword and shield
    Make victory sure,
    Make Satan yield.

4. God and his saints invite;
Hell warns with dreadful voice:
Life, death, all things unite,
To press thy timely choice.
    List to that call—
    On Jesus' side—
    Trust now thine all
    In him above.

THE POLAR STAR.

2.
Stranger on a rocky strand,
Longing for thy fatherland,
Thro' the gathering clouds that rise,
Veiling thy natal skies;
Look beyond, there's hope for thee,
Dawning o'er a tranquil sea:
Softly it smiles, though distant far,
The beautiful polar star.

3.
Lonely watcher, pale with grief,
Thou shalt find a sweet relief,
Though thy tears unheeded fall,
Jesus will count them all;
Look beyond, there's joy for thee,
Breaking o'er a troubled sea;
Softly it smiles, though distant far
The beautiful polar star.

IN THAT HAPPY LAND.

Arranged by W. H. DOANE.

1. We are trav'ling home to heav'n a-bove, Will you go with us?
We are trav'ling home to heaven a-bove, Will you go with us?

CHORUS.
O, that's the heaven that I'm bound for, That's the heaven I love;
O, that's the heaven I'm long-ing for, That's the heaven for me.

2 Companions, will you go with us,
 Will you go with us?
 Companions, will you go with us
 To that happy land?

3 Dear parents, will you go with us,
 Will you go with us?
 Dear parents, will you go with us
 To that happy land?

4 We'll meet, dear children, in that land,
 In that happy land;
 We'll meet, dear children, in that land,
 In that happy land.

5 We'll meet, dear parents, in that land,
 In that happy land:
 We'll meet, dear parents, in that land,
 In that happy land.

6 Our Saviour's hand will lead us on,
 Will you go with us?
 Our Saviour's hand will lead us on
 To that happy land.

MINE THE CROSS.

Words by Miss FANNY CROSBY. T. E. P.

1. Mine the cross, and thine the glory, Thou hast suffered once for me;
Let my life be calm or clouded, I can trust it, Lord, to thee.
Let me feel the sweet assurance Of thy presence always near,
Grant me on-ly this, my Father, And my soul can nev-er fear.

2. All I am thy grace has made me,
   All I am I owe to thee,
I can only thank and praise thee
   For a love so pure and free.
Self-denying, persevering,
   Where thy blessed feet have led,
May I follow, daily growing
   Up to thee, my living head.

3. Mine the cross, and thine the glory,
   Thou hast borne it once for me;
Help me bear with Christian meekness
   Every trial sent by thee.
On thy strength alone relying,
   With thy lamp to cheer my way,
Leaning on the staff of mercy,
   I will labor, trust, and pray.

UP AND DOING.

51

Words by Mrs. M. A. KIDDER.

2. Let us save the soul benighted,
   Let us turn the wayward feet
   From the paths of sin and darkness
   To the pastures fair and sweet.
   CHO.—Up and doing, etc.

3. Let us soothe the broken-hearted,
   Pointing them to joys on high:
   Let us help the poor and needy,
   Let us heed the orphan's cry.
   CHO.—Up and doing, etc.

4. Tenderly, oh, let us gather,
   From the storm and from the cold,
   All the little lambs, that Jesus
   May protect them in his fold.
   CHO.—Up and doing, etc.

THE ANGEL'S WELCOME.

Rev. R. LOWRY.

1. My rest is in heav-en, my rest is not here, Then why should I
   Be hushed, my dark spir-it, the worst that can come, [Omit ----
   murmur when tri-als are near?]
   But shortens thy journey, and hastens thee home.

Then the an-gels will come, with their mu-sic will come, With music, sweet music to wel-come me home; In the bright gates of crys-tal the shin-ing ones will stand, And sing me a wel-come to their own na-tive land.

2. It is not for me to be seeking my bliss,
   Or building my hopes in a region like this;
   I look for a city that hands have not piled,
   I pant for a country by sin undefiled.—CHORUS.

THE ANGEL'S WELCOME.

3. Afflictions may press me, they cannot destroy—
One glimpse of his love turns them all into joy:
And the bitterest tears, if he smile but on them,
Like dew in the sunshine, grow diamond and gem.—Cho.

4. Let trial and danger my progress oppose,
They only make heaven more sweet at its close;
Come joy, or come sorrow, whate'er may befall,
An hour with my Saviour will make up for all.—Cho.

COME TO JESUS, LITTLE ONE.

Words by Rev. E. TURNEY, D.D.

1. Come to Jesus, little one; Come to Jesus now;
Humbly at his gracious throne In submission bow.
At his feet confess your sin, Seek forgiveness there,
For his blood can make you clean, He will hear your prayer.

2. Seek his face without delay;
Give him now your heart;
Tarry not, but, while you may,
Choose the better part.
Come to Jesus, little one;
Come to Jesus now:
Humbly at his gracious throne
In submission bow.

PRESS ONWARD.

VANALSTYNE.

1. Press on-ward, press on-ward, tho' oft your way is dark, With courage and vigor press onward to the mark: Oh, lay aside the weight of sin, and now with all your might begin. Press onward, press onward where duty leads the way, Press onward, press onward where duty leads the way.

2. Press onward, press onward, whatever may oppose,
The Saviour will help you to conquer all your foes;
Remember former things no more, but reaching forth to things before.
Press onward, press onward, where duty leads the way.

3. Press onward, press onward, a rest remains for you,
Be watchful, be faithful, your glorious home in view;
Be swift your heavenly race to run, nor weary till your crown is won.
Press onward, press onward, where duty leads the way.

3. When evening shadows o'er me creep,
   Thine eye can see;
   When on my pillow calm I sleep,
   Thine eye can see;
   I thank thee for thy watchful care,
   How sweet thy tender love to share,
   And know that every grief I bear
   Thine eye can see. Cho.

4. If I would serve thee day by day,
   Thine eye can see;
   If from thy pleasant paths I stray,
   Thine eye can see;
   Oh, take my heart, my will subdue,
   And may I ever keep in view,
   That all I think and all I do
   Thine eye can see.

CLIMBING UP ZION'S HILL.

From the "Singing Pilgrim." By permission of P. PHILLIPS.

2. I know I'm but a little child,
    My strength will not protect me;
   But then I am the Saviour's lamb,
    And he will not neglect me.
   Then all the time I'll try to climb
    This holy hill of Zion,
   For I am sure the way is pure,
    And on it comes " no lion."
        SOLO.—I'm climbing, &c.

3. Then come with me, we'll upward go,
    And climb this hill together,
   And as we walk, we'll sweetly talk,
    And sing as we go thither.
   Then mount up still God's holy hill,
    Till we reach the pearly portals,
   Where raptured tongues proclaim the
        songs
   Of the shining-robed Immortals. SOLO.

I'M GOING TO BE A SOLDIER. 57

Spirited.   Words by Mrs. H. E. BROWN. By Permission.

2. The foes that will assail me,
   Are subtle, fierce, and strong;
The war that they are waging
   Will deadly be, and long;
But I've a well-tried helmet,
   A sword and trusty shield,
To quench the fiery arrows
   That Satan's hand may wield.—Cho.

3. I know I'm small and feeble,
   But Jesus is my head;
He's wise and strong and able,
   To triumph he will lead;
And when beneath his banner
   I've gained the victor's crown,
With one long, loud hosanna,
   I'll lay my armor down.—Cho.

58. GO AND WORK.

2. Go and work, nor idly stand
   On the living fountain's brink,
   Pining in a desert land,
     Souls are thirsty, give them drink;
   Question not if duty lead,
     Take the cross, and bear our part,
   Where we find a lamb to feed
     Do it with a loving heart.—Cho.

3. Be our mission where it will,
     Sow the seed, and wait the rain;
   If we follow Jesus still
     We shall never toil in vain.
   Look abroad, the fields are white,
     Lo! the harvest time is near;
   Labor with the morning light,
     Soon the reapers will appear—Cho.

HOME OF THE BLEST

T. E. P.

2. Far away beyond the shadows
   Of this weary vale of tears,
  There the tide of bliss is sweeping
   Through the bright and changeless year;
  Oh, I long to be with Jesus,
   In the mansions of the blest,
  "Where the wicked cease from troubling,
   And the weary are at rest."

3. They are launching on the river,
   From the calm and quiet shore,
  And they soon will bear my spirit
   Where the weary sigh no more;
  For the tide is swiftly flowing,
   And I long to greet the blest,
  "Where the wicked cease from troubling,
   And the weary are at rest."

THE ORPHAN WANDERER.

T. E. PERKINS.

THE ORPHAN WANDERER. 61

2. Torn from parental love, guide of her youth,
Who now will gently breathe lessons of truth?
Who lead her trembling steps home to the skies,
Where sorrow never comes, hope never dies?
Lovingly, tenderly, teach her to pray;
Tell of the better land, show her the way.
Hark! 'tis thy Saviour speaks kindly to thee,
All you may do for her is done for me. *Cho.*

62. OVER ON THE OTHER SIDE.

Words by Mrs. M. A. KIDDER.   Arranged from W. H. DOANE.

1. On-ly just a-cross the riv-er, O-ver on the oth-er side,
2. On-ly just a-cross the riv-er, Are the friends we loved be-low,

Where the an-gels are in wait-ing, And the pure in heart a-bide;
Clad in pure and spot-less gar-ments, That are whit-er than the snow;

Where there is no pain or sor-row To in-trude on heavenly rest,
They have braved cold Jordan's billows, And have passed thro' death's alarms,

On-ly just a-cross the riv-er, Stand the man-sions of the blest.
And are safe, for-ev-er safe, With-in the Sav-iour's lov-ing arms.

Chorus.

On-ly just a-cross the riv-er, Where the saints are pass-ing o-ver,

On-ly just a-cross the riv-er, O-ver on the oth-er side.

OVER ON THE OTHER SIDE.

3. Only just across the river,
 Where the hills of glory shine,
There the pearly gates stand open
 Wide that lead to joys divine.
There the tree of life is blooming,
 And the living waters glide,
Only just across the river,
 Over on the other side.—Chorus.

4. Only just across the river
 Are the robes of spotless white;
Only just across the river
 Are the crowns of glory bright,
And the saints and angels joining
 In the songs of one accord,
Only just across the river,
 Sing the praises of the Lord.—Chorus.

PILGRIM, WATCH AND PRAY.

Words by Miss FANNY CROSBY.   T. E. P.

1. Soft-ly on the breath of evening Comes the ten-der sigh of day;
 Lonely heart, by sorrow lad-en, 'Tis the time to pray. Wea-ry pil-grim,
 cease thy mourning, Weary pilgrim, cease thy mourning, Rest beyond forever.

2. Pearl-y dews like tears are fall-ing Gent-ly on the sleeping flowers,
 Stars like angel eyes are beaming From celestial bowers. Wea-ry, etc.

3. 'Tis the hour where hallowed feelings
 Chase our doubts and fears away;
'Tis the hour for calm devotion,
 Pilgrim, watch and pray.—Cho.

4. Though temptations dark oppress thee,
 Jesus guides thee on thy way;
He will hear thy lightest whisper,
 Pilgrim, watch and pray.—Cho.

EASTER ANTHEM.

C. G. ALLEN.

1. Christ the Lord is risen to-day, Sons of men and an-gels say: Raise your joys and triumphs high, Sing, ye heavens, and earth re-ply. Love's re-deem-ing work is done, Fought the fight, the vic-tory won: Je-sus' ag-o-ny is o'er, Dark-ness veils the earth no more.

2. Vain the stone, the watch, the seal,
Christ has burst the gates of hell;
Death in vain forbids him rise,
Christ hath opened paradise.
Soar we now where Christ hath led,
Following our exalted Head:
Made like him, like him we rise;
Ours the cross, the grave, the skies.

SPEAK FOR JESUS.

T. E. P.

1. Brethren, let us speak for Jesus, Tell the world his power to save;
   He who gave his life our ransom, Rose and triumph'd o'er the grave.

Chorus.
Glory, glory, joys eternal Wait us on that happy shore;
There we'll sing his praise for ev - er, When we meet to part no more;
There we'll sing his praise for ev - er, When we meet to part no more.

2. If the flame of zeal is burning,
   If it glow from heart to heart,
   In the blessed cause of Jesus,
   We shall try to do our part.
   Cho.—Glory, glory, &c.

3. We must live and work for Jesus,
   Whatsoe'er we find to do,
   In the vineyard of our master,
   Let us with our might pursue.
   Cho.—Glory, glory, &c.

BEAUTIFUL VALE OF REST.   67

3. The joys of earth, how soon they fade!
    Beautiful vale of rest;
  Like morning dew or evening shade;
    Beautiful vale of rest:
  Yet, when we reach thy golden strand,
  Our gentle Saviour's promised land,
  We'll sing with all the angel band,
    Happy vale of rest.

4. Oh, who would dwell forever here,
    Beautiful vale of rest;
  With joy, unfading joy, so near,
    Beautiful vale of rest.
  Oh, may I live that I may wear
  A starry crown for ever there,
  And breathe thy sweet and balmy air,
    Happy vale of rest.

DENNIS. S. M.
Arranged from H. G. NAGELI.

1. I love thy kingdom, Lord—The house of thine abode,—
The church our blest Redeemer saved With his own precious blood.

2. I love thy church, O God!
    Her walls before thee stand,
  Dear as the apple of thine eye,
    And graven on thy hand.

3. For her my tears shall fall;
    For her my prayers ascend;
  To her my cares and toils be given,
    Till toils and cares shall end.

4. Beyond my highest joy
    I prize her heavenly ways;
  Her sweet communion, solemn vows,
    Her hymns of love and praise.

5. Sure as thy truth shall last,
    To Zion shall be given
  The brightest glories earth can yield,
    And brighter bliss of heaven.

2.
We've girded on our armor bright,
  Battling for the Lord!
Our captain's word our strength and might,
  Battling for the Lord!—Cho.

3.
We'll stand like heroes on the field,
  Battling for the Lord!
And nobly fight but never yield,
  Battling for the Lord!—Cho.

4.
Though sin and death our way oppose,
  Battling for the Lord!
Through grace we'll conquer all our foes,
  Battling for the Lord!—Cho.

5.
And when our glorious war is o'er,
  Battling for the Lord!
We'll shout salvation evermore,
  Battling for the Lord!—Cho.

WHEN THE MORNING LIGHT.

Rev. R. LOWRY.

1. When the morning light drives away the night, With the sun so bright and full,
   And the day of rest lightens every breast, I'll a-way to the Sabbath school;
2. On the frosty dawn of a winter's morn, When the earth is wrapped in snow,
   Or the summer breeze plays around the trees, To the Sabbath school I go;

For 'tis there we all a-gree, All with hap-py hearts and free, And I
When the ho-ly day has come, And the Sab-bath breakers roam, I de-

Girls. *Boys.*
love to oar-ly be At the Sab-bath-School; I'll a-way! a-way!
-light to leave my home For the Sab-bath-school; I'll a-way, &c.

Girls. *Boys.* *All.*
I'll a-way! a-way! I'll a-way to Sab-bath-School.

3. In the class I meet with the friends I greet,
   At the time of morning prayer;
   And our hearts we raise in a hymn of praise,
   For 'tis always pleasant there.
       In the book of holy truth,
       Full of counsel and reproof,
       We behold the guide of youth,
       At the Sabbath school. I'll away, &c.

4. May the dews of grace fill the hallow'd place,
   And the sunshine never fail,
   While each blooming rose which in memory grows
   Shall a sweet perfume exhale.
       When we mingle here no more,
       But have met on Jordan's shore,
       We will talk of moments o'er
       At the Sabbath school. I'll away, &c.

70 I'M KNEELING AT THE DOOR.

Words by Mrs. LYDIA C. BAXTER. Music by T. E. PERKINS.

2. None ever empty turned away,
   Who truly sought thy face:
   And I, my Saviour, come to-day,
   To seek thy pardoning grace.

I'M KNEELING AT THE DOOR. 71

Thy precious blood is all my plea:
This, can my soul restore;
Wilt thou in mercy speak to me,
I'm kneeling at the door.

3. And when the ransomed millions stand
On Zion's flowery hill,
With palms of victory in their hand,
Waiting their Master's will:
Oh, may I bear the living green,
And that dear name above,
Whose love the sinner did redeem,
While kneeling at the door.

GOD BLESS OUR SCHOOL.

Words and Music by Rev. ALFRED TAYLOR. By permission.

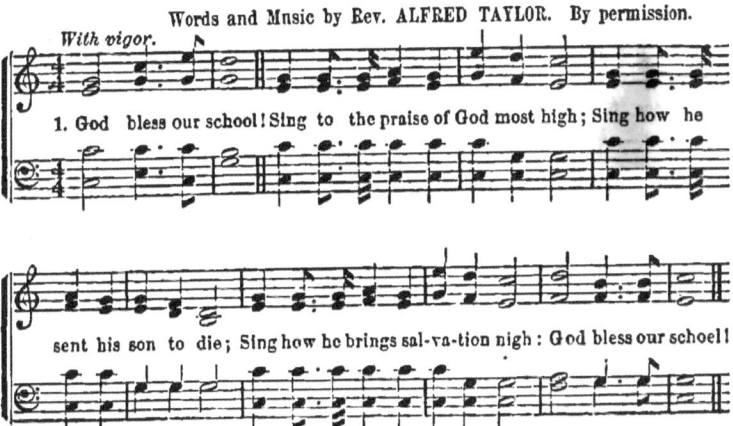

1. God bless our school! Sing to the praise of God most high; Sing how he sent his son to die; Sing how he brings sal-va-tion nigh: God bless our school!

2. God bless our school!
Bring all the wandering children in,
Bring all the heirs of death and sin,
Bring them immortal life to win;
God bless our school!

3. God bless our school!
Teach us the word of truth to know,
Teach us in Christian strength to grow,
Teach us to serve thee here below!
God bless our school!

4. God bless our school!
Fill all our hearts with heavenly grace,
Lead us in love to that blest place
Where we shall see our Saviour's face.
God bless our school!

BY-AND-BYE.

2.
We shall find a glorious treasure,
By-and-bye, by-and-bye,
In the golden fields of pleasure,
By-and-bye, by-and-bye.
If we sow in faith and meekness,
We shall reap, we shall reap,
Where the heart is never weary,
And the eyes never weep.
Cho.—We shall rest, &c.

3.
We are going, we are going,
By-and-bye, by-and-bye,
Where ambrosial fruits are growing,
By-and-bye, by-and-bye.

We shall meet our friends departed,
On the shore, on the shore,
And our souls again united,
There to part nevermore.
Cho.—We shall rest, &c.

4.
There with rapture we'll adore Him,
By-and-bye, by-and-bye,
And we'll cast our crowns before Him,
By-and-bye, by-and-bye.
In the sunny vales of Eden
We shall be, we shall be,
And we'll sing through endless ages,
Grace is free, grace is free.
Cho.—We shall rest, &c.

JESUS PAID IT ALL.

T. E. PERKINS.

1. Nothing ei-ther great or small, Remains for me to do; Jesus died and paid it all,—Yes, all the debt I owe. Je-sus paid it all,—all the debt I owe, Je-sus died and paid it all—Yes, all the debt I owe.

2 When he from his lofty throne,
Stooped down to do and die;
Everything was fully done;
Yes, " finished !" was his cry.
Cho.—Jesus paid it all, &c.

3 Weary, working, plodding one!
O, wherefore toil you so?
Cease your " doing;" all was done
Ages long ago.
Cho.—Jesus paid it all, &c.

4 Till to Jesus' work you cling,
Alone by simple faith,
"Doing" is a deadly thing,
" Doing," ends in death.
Cho.—Jesus paid it all, &c.

5 Cast your deadly " doing " down,
Down all at Jesus' feet ;
Stand in Him, in Him alone,
Glorious and complete,
Cho.—Jesus paid it all, &c.

74 COME TO THE MANGER.

Words by G. W. YOUNG, Esq. Music by J. T. GRAPE.

2. Oh, come the Manger—the angel is winging
The air, while his tidings are sounding abroad:
And a legion of heavenly choristers singing
Good will to the nations, and glory to God!
Hast thou not a word for the joyous meeting,
No song in that anthem of glory to share?
Awake from thy slumbers, to join in their greeting,
And come to the Manger—for Jesus is there!

COME TO THE MANGER.

2. Oh, come to Manger—the shepherds, obeying
   The herald of glory, are there even now:
Their fervent petitions of gratitude paying,
   And pleading their fealty and making their vow.
Hast thou no allegiance to offer before him,
   No vows of affection, no penitent prayer?
Awake from thy slumbers, prepare to adore him,
   And come to the Manger—for Jesus is there!

4. Oh, come to the Manger—the star is yet shining,
   Undimmed by a cloud, uneclipsed by the morn;
Like curtains of silver, its radiance inclining,
   To shelter the couch where the Saviour was born,
It shines to invite, to assure, to direct thee,
   'Tis an omen of Mercy—no longer forbear;
The Shepherds, the Magi, the Angels expect thee,
   Come, come to the Manger—for Jesus is there!

JESUS, TENDER SAVIOUR.

H. N. WHITNEY. By permission.

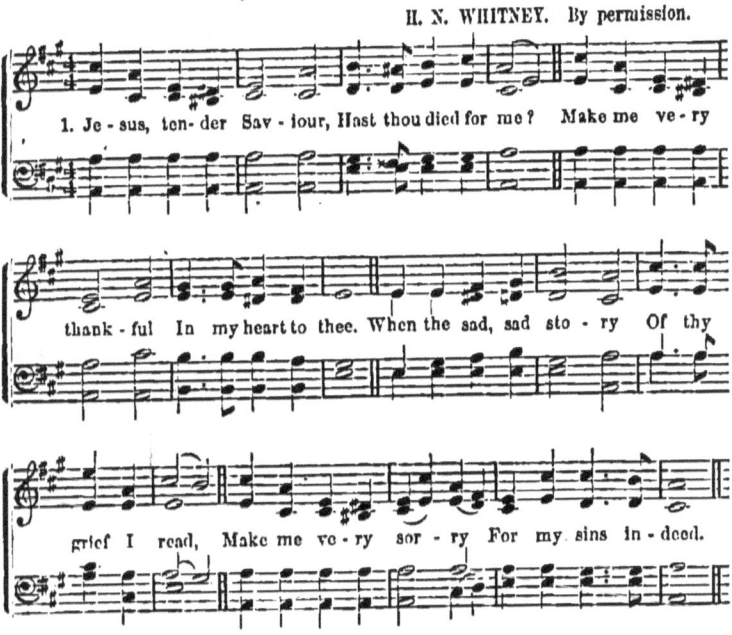

1. Je-sus, ten-der Sav-iour, Hast thou died for me? Make me ve-ry thank-ful In my heart to thee. When the sad, sad sto-ry Of thy grief I read, Make me ve-ry sor-ry For my sins in-deed.

2. Now I know thou lovest,
     And dost plead for me,
   Make me very thankful
     In my pray'rs to thee.

3. Soon, I hope, in glory,
     At thy side to stand:
   Make me fit to meet thee
     In that happy land.

3. Who is he who stands and weeps
At the grave where Laz'rus sleeps?
4. Who is he in deep distress,
Fasting in the wilderness?
5. Lo! at midnight, who is he
Prays in dark Gethsemane?

6. Who is he in Calv'ry's throes
Asks for blessings on His foes?
7. Who is he that, from the grave,
Comes to heal, and help, and save?
8. Who is he that on yon throne
Rules the world of light alone?

REDEEMING LOVE. 77

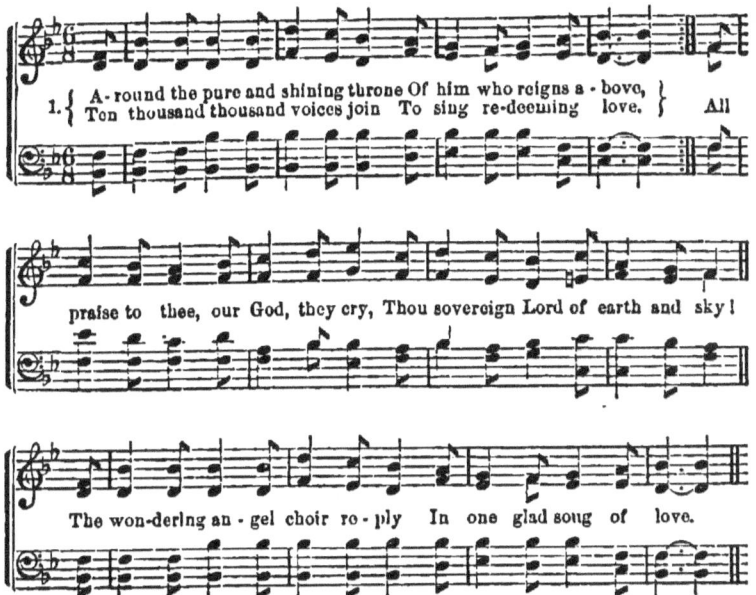

2. There kings and prophets, ancient sires
　　Of Judah's chosen race,
　Before their great Deliverer stand,
　　And view his smiling face;
　They bow adoring at his feet,
　Then strike their harps with joy complete;
　They died in faith, and now they meet
　　To sing redeeming love.

3. There every nation, kindred, tongue,
　　Exalt the Saviour's name,
　With loud, triumphant shouts of joy
　　His mighty works proclaim;
　And in our Father's mansion bright,
　Whose gates are open day and night,
　Are children robed in spotless white,
　　Who sing redeeming love.

4. We long to fold our starry wings
　　Among that saintly band,
　That round the pure and shining throne
　　With crowns of glory stand.
　Oh, may we gain that peaceful shore,
　When earthly storms and cares are o'er,
　With happy children gone before
　　To sing redeeming love.

DARK IS THE NIGHT.

Words by FANNY CROSBY. Music by T. E. P.

1. Dark is the night, and cold the wind is blowing,
   Where shall I go, or whither fly for refuge?
   Nearer and nearer comes the breakers' roar—
   Hide me, my Father, till the storm is o'er!

   Chorus.
   With his loving hand to guide, let the clouds above me roll,
   I can brave the wildest storm with his glory in my soul,
   1st time. And the billows in their fury dash around me,
   [Omit..]
   2d time. I can sing amidst the tempest—Praise the Lord!

2. Dark is the night, but cheering is the promise:
   He will go with me o'er the troubled wave;
   Safe he will lead me through the pathless waters,
   Jesus, the mighty one and strong to save.—Cho.

3. Dark is the night, but lo! the day is breaking,
   Onward my bark, unfurl thy every sail;
   Now at the helm I see my Father standing,
   Soon will my anchor drop within the vale.—Cho.

JEWELS.

G. F. R. From "Chapel Gems," by permission of ROOT & CADY.

2.
He will gather, he will gather
 The gems for his kingdom;
All the pure ones, all the bright ones,
 His lov'd and his own.—Cho.

3.
Little children, little children,
 Who love their Redeemer,
Are the jewels, precious jewels,
 His lov'd and his own.—Cho.

COMFORT ME.

Words by FANNY. Music by W. H. PETTIBONE.

1. Weak and sin-ful, O my Fa-ther, Hop-ing, trust-ing on-ly thee, Fold thy lov-ing arms a-round me, Sav-iour, thou hast died for me. Com-fort me, Com-fort me, Bless-ed Sav-iour, com-fort me.

2. Standing at the door of mercy,
   Lord, I wait a smile from thee;
   Rich and boundless are thy blessings,
   Surely there is one for me.
   Comfort me, etc.

3. Thou, my life, my only treasure,
   Let me give myself to thee,
   Let me drink the healing fountain;
   There is comfort still for me.
   Comfort me, etc.

4. Thou hast rolled away my burden,
   Praise forever, praise to thee;
   Blessed pardon, now I feel it,
   Thou hast spoken, Lord, to me.
   I am free, I am free,
   Saviour thou dost comfort me.

WATCHING, HOPING, PRAYING. 81.

Words by FANNY CROSBY. Music by T. E. PERKINS.

1. Do we thirst for liv-ing wa-ter, In a des-ert pin-ing?
Do we, walk-ing here in dark-ness, Feel our strength de-clin-ing?
In the gold-en fields of pleas-ure, By the crys-tal riv-er,
With the faith-ful gone be-fore us Soon we rest for ev-er.

2. Jesus feels our every trial,
   In his love abiding,
   Bear the cross, and wait with patience,
   All to him confiding.
   In the golden fields of pleasure,
   By the crystal river,
   With the faithful gone before us
   Soon we rest for ever.

3. Look beyond life's troubled ocean,
   Joy by faith surveying,
   Press we onward to the haven,
   Watching, hoping, praying.
   In the golden field of pleasure,
   By the crystal river,
   With the faithful gone before us
   Soon we rest for ever.

82 COME TO THE FOUNTAIN.

Words by FANNY CROSBY.   Music by W. H. DOANE.

1. Come to the fount-ain of mer-cy and live, Come, and a par-don re-ceive; Drink of the wa-ter that Je-sus will give, Free-ly to those that be-lieve; { Weary and burdened with sorrow, Learn of the meek and the lowly, Sweet is the mes-sage to thee, Come, heavy-lad-en to [OMIT.] } me. Come to the clear flowing riv-er, Drink of its wa-ter for ev-er, Hun-gry and thirst-y, oh, nev-er, Blessed are they that be-lieve!

COME TO THE FOUNTAIN.

2. Happy the nation whose God is the Lord;
    Hearing in meekness and love
  Counsels of wisdom and truth in his word,
    Looking for comfort above;
  He is their rock and salvation,
    He is their strength and their song,
  Onward from glory to glory,
    Leading them gently along.—Cho.

3. Look unto Jesus, ye regions of earth,
    Victor of death and the grave,
  Though he was humble, and lowly his birth,
    He is the mighty to save.
  Why should we wander in darkness ?
    Why to the world should we cling ?
  Hope, like a bird, is before us,
    Pluming her beautiful wing.—Cho.

AZMON. C. M. — GLASER.

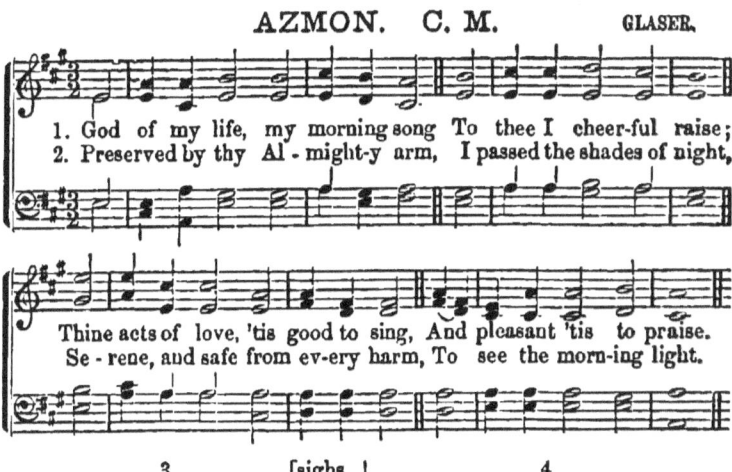

1. God of my life, my morning song To thee I cheerful raise;
   Thine acts of love, 'tis good to sing, And pleasant 'tis to praise.
2. Preserved by thy Almighty arm, I passed the shades of night,
   Serene, and safe from every harm, To see the morning light.

3.   [sighs,
While numbers spend their night in
  And restless pains and woes,
In gentle sleep I close my eyes,
  And wake from sweet repose.

4.
Oh, let the same Almighty care
  Through all this day attend;
From every danger, every snare,
  My heedless steps defend.

THE ONE PETITION.

1.
Father, whate'er of earthly bliss
  Thy sovereign will denies,
Accepted at thy throne of grace,
  Let this petition rise;

2.
Give me a calm, a thankful heart,
  From every murmur free:

The blessings of thy grace impart
  And make me live to thee.

3.
Let the sweet hope that I am thine,
  My life and death attend;
Thy presence through my journey shine,
  And crown my journey's end.

JESUS IS HERE.

From "Singing Pilgrim," by permission of PHILIP PHILLIPS.

1. O, come to Jesus now, Jesus is here, Jesus is here;
All low before him bow, Jesus is here, Jesus is here;
Too many go a-way, Too many still de-lay, Though
Jesus bids them stay; Jesus is here, Jesus is here.

2. O, come this place within, Jesus is here, Jesus is here;
He sees you full of sin, Jesus is here, Jesus is here;
He knows you when you come, Poor, wretched and undone, Seeking
Him and Him a-lone; Jesus is here, Jesus is here.

3 Come, then, to Jesus now,
  Jesus is here, Jesus is here;
All near him lowly bow,
  Jesus is here, Jesus is here.
O, ye that feel your sin,
And coming long have been,
Now find your rest in him;
  Jesus is here, Jesus is here.

4 O, come to Jesus now,
  Jesus is here, Jesus is here;
Old and young together bow,
  Jesus is here, Jesus is here.
O, what a glorious thing,
Sin's weary load to bring,
And lose it while we sing:
  Jesus is here, Jesus is here.

BEATUIFUL HOME ABOVE. 85

Words by Mrs. M. A. KIDDER. Music by T. E. PERKINS.

1. O, how my spir-it longs for thee, Beau-ti-ful home a-bove! Where
2. To reach thee safe I dai-ly pray, Beau-ti-ful home a-bove! And

I may rest, from sorrow free, Beautiful home a-bove! With-in the gold-en
trav-el in the toilsome way, Beautiful home a-bove! My wea-ry feet are

gates of light, Arrayed in garments pure and white, I'll walk with an-gels
bruised and sore, But Je-sus' feet were bruised be-fore, To bring me to the

Chorus.

fair and bright, In my home a-bove. Beau-ti-ful home a-bove,
o-pen door Of my home a-bove. Beau-ti-ful home, &c.

Beau-ti-ful home a-bove—Oh, come and take me, Sav-iour, come: I

love my beau-ti-ful home.

3 Thy shining walls by faith I see,
  Beautiful home above!
The mansions fair prepared for me,
  Beautiful home above!
Oh, let me keep my longing eyes,
Intently fixed upon the prize,
Till angels bear me to the skies,
  In my home above.—CHORUS.

86. SHALL WE KNOW EACH OTHER?

Rev. R. LOWRY.

SHALL WE KNOW EACH OTHER? 87

2. Yes, my earth-worn soul rejoices,
    And my weary heart grows light,
   For the thrilling angel voices,
    And the angel faces bright,
   That shall welcome us in heaven,
    Are the loved of long ago,
   And to them 'tis kindly given
    Thus their mortal friends to know.
     We shall know, &c.

3. Oh! ye weary, heavy-laden,.
    Droop not, faint not by the way;
   Ye shall join the loved departed
    In the land of perfect day.
   Harp-strings touched by angel fingers
    Murmur in my raptured ear;
   Evermore their sweet tone lingers,
    We shall know each other there.
     We shall know, &c.

THE LORD IS MY SHEPHERD.

Chant.

1. The Lord | is my | shepherd;
   I | shall — | not — | want.

2. He maketh me to lie down | in green | pastures:
   He leadeth me be- | side the | still — | waters.

3. He re- | storeth my | soul:
   He leadeth me in the path of righteousness | for his | name's — | sake.

4. Yes, though I walk through the valley of the shadow of death, I will | fear no | evil:
   For thou art with me: thy rod and thy | staff, they | comfort | me.

5. Thou preparest a table before me in the presence | of mine | enemies.
   Thou anointest my head with oil: my | cup — | runneth | over.

6. Surely goodness and mercy shall follow me all the | days of · my | life.
   And I will dwell in the | house of the | Lord for- | ever.

DAWN, O GOLDEN GLORY.

Words by Mrs. M. A. KIDDER.

1. Tell me, watchman on the steep, While I wait and while I weep,
Cho. Dawn, O gold-en glo-ry, dawn; Hasten, sweet mil-lennium morn:
Will the night soon dis-ap-pear? Is the day-light al-most here?
Bright ce-les-tial Sun, a-rise O'er the por-tals of the skies.
Brother, lift your tear-ful eyes, See the Sun of glo-ry rise;
Soon his bless-ed rays di-vine O'er a ransom'd world will shine.

Christian. 2. Tell me, shepherd of the sheep,
 While I wait, and while I weep,
 Can I fly the storm and cold,
 May I reach the heavenly fold?
Shepherd. Brother, through the stormy way
 Christ, your Shepherd, once did stray,
 Now his glory you may share
 In the mansions bright and fair.—Cho.

Christian. 2. Tell me, reaper, as you reap,
 While I wait, and while I weep,
 Is the harvest nearly past,
 May I yet my sickle cast?
Reaper. Brother, see, the grain is white;
 Reap, oh reap, while yet there's light;
 Soon the reaper's rest shall come,
 Soon we'll sing our harvest home.—Cho.

THE LAMBS OF THE UPPER FOLD. 89

B. R. H. From "Chapel Gems," by permission.

1. 'Mid the pastures green of the bless-ed isles, Where nev-er is heat or cold, Where the light of life Is the Shepherds's smile, Are the Lambs of the Up-per Fold. Where the lil-ies blos-som in fade-less spring, And nev-er a heart grows old, Where the glad new song is the song they sing, Are the Lambs of the Up-per Fold. Fold. Lambs of the Up-per Fold, Lambs of the Up-per Fold.

2. There are ti-ny mounds where the hopes of earth Were laid 'neath the tear-wet mold, But the light that paled at the strick-en hearth Was joy to the Up-per Fold. Oh, the white stone bear-eth a new name now, That nev-er on earth was told, And the ten-der Shep-herd doth guard with care The Lambs of the Up-per Fold. Fold. Lambs, etc.

EVEN ME.

T. E. Perkins.

1. Lord, I hear of show'rs of blessings Thou art scatt'ring full and free; Show'rs the thirst-y land re-fresh-ing, Let some drop-pings fall on me!— E-ven me, E-ven me! Let some droppings fall on me.

2. Pass me not, O God, our Fa-ther! Sin-ful though my heart may be; Thou might'st leave me, but the ra-ther Let thy mer-cy light on me!— E-ven me, E-ven me! Let thy mer-cy light on me.

3. Pass me not, O gracious Saviour!
Let me live and cling to thee!
For I'm longing for thy favor;
Whilst thou art calling, oh, call me—Even me.

4. Pass me not, O mighty Spirit!
Thou canst make the blind to see;
Witnesser of Jesus' merit!
Speak some word of power to me—Even me.

5. Have I long in sin been sleeping—
Long been slighting, grieving thee!
Has the world my heart been keeping!
Oh! forgive, and rescue me!—Even me.

6. Love of God—so pure and changeless;
Blood of Christ—so rich, so free;
Grace of God—so strong and boundless,
Magnify it all in me!—Even me.

HEBER. C. M.

GEORGE KINGSLEY. By permission.

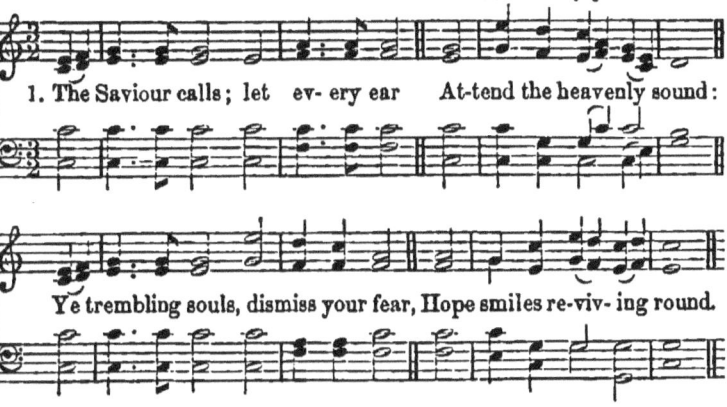

1. The Saviour calls; let every ear
Attend the heavenly sound:
Ye trembling souls, dismiss your fear,
Hope smiles reviving round.

2. For every thirsty, longing heart,
Here streams of bounty flows,
And life, and health, and bliss impart,
To banish mortal woe.

3. Ye sinners! come; 'tis mercy's voice;
The gracious call obey:
Mercy invites to heavenly joys,—
And can you yet delay?

4. Dear Saviour! draw reluctant hearts;
To thee let sinners fly,
And take the bliss that love imparts,
And drink, and never die.

THE LORD'S PRAYER.
TALLIS.

1. Our Father who art in heaven, hallowed | be thy | name;
2. Thy kingdom come; thy will be done, on | earth, ·· as it | is in | heaven.
3. Give us this day our | daily | bread;
4. And forgive us our trespasses, as we forgive | them that | trespass a- | gainst us.
5. And lead us not into temptation, but deliver | us from | evil;
6. For thine is the kingdom, and the power, and the glory, for- | ever ·· and | ever. A- | men.

SINGING FOR JESUS.

PHILIP PHILLIPS. By Permission.

2. Singing for Jesus glad hymns of devotion,
Lifting the soul on her pinions of love;
Dropping a word or a thought by the wayside,
Telling of rest in the mansions above.

SINGING FOR JESUS. 93

Music may soften where language would fail us,
Feelings long buried 'twill often restore,
Tones that were breathed from the lips of departed,
How we revere them when they are no more!

3. Singing for Jesus, my blessed Redeemer,
God of the pilgrims, for thee I will sing,
When o'er the billows of time I am wafted,
Still with thy praise shall eternity ring.
Glory to God for the prospect before me,
Soon shall my spirit transported ascend;
Singing for Jesus, oh, blissful employment,
Loud hallelujahs that never will end.

FULLNESS IN CHRIST.

Words by Mrs. E. M. HALL. Music by J. T. GRAPE.

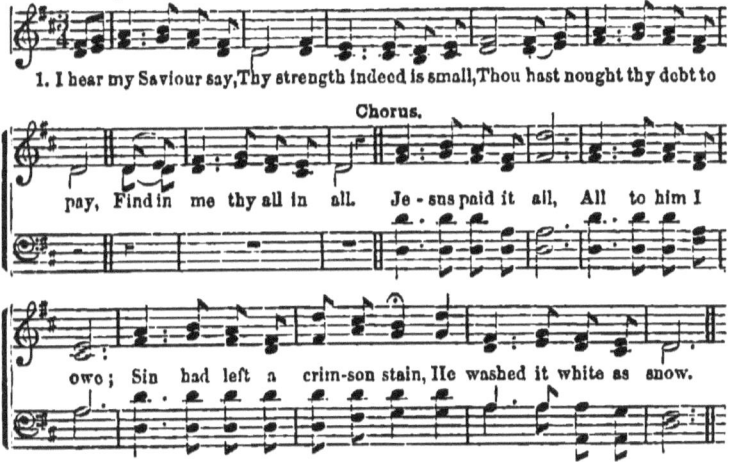

1. I hear my Saviour say, Thy strength indeed is small, Thou hast nought thy debt to pay, Find in me thy all in all. Je-sus paid it all, All to him I owe; Sin had left a crim-son stain, He washed it white as snow.

2. Yea, nothing good have I,
  Whereby thy grace to claim;
  I'll wash my garments white
  In the blood of Calvary's Lamb.—Cho.

3. And now complete in him,
  My robe his righteousness,
  Close sheltered 'neath his side,
  I am divinely blest.—Cho.

4. When from my dying bed
  My ransomed soul shall rise,
  Jesus paid it all,
  Shall rend the vaulted skies.—Cho.

5. And when before the throne
  I stand in him complete,
  I'll lay my trophies down,
  All down at Jesus' feet.—Cho.

94 WE LOVE THE SABBATH SCHOOL.

Words by Miss FANNY J. CROSBY.

1. We are a group of happy children, Full of glee, full of glee, We are a group of happy children, We love the Sabbath school; Swiftly the moments wing their flight, Making our hearts with pleasure bright. We are a group of happy children, We love the Sabbath school.

2. Heard ye the voice of love and mercy,
   Joyful sound, Joyful sound,
   Heard ye the voice of love and mercy,
   Come from the Sabbath school.
   Angels above that song repeat,
   Casting their crowns at Jesus' feet,
   Sweet is the voice of love and mercy
   Heard in the Sabbath school.

3. Come, let us give our hearts to Jesus,
   One and all, one and all,
   Come, let us give our hearts to Jesus,
   Now in the Sabbath school.
   Soon will the day of life be o'er,
   Then we shall meet to part no more!
   Yes, we will give our hearts to Jesus,
   Now in the Sabbath school.

THE BANNER OF JESUS.

Words by FANNY CROSBY. *Music by T. E. PERKINS.*

1. Like the he-roes who gave us the land that we love, We will fight for our home and our coun-try a-bove; And the ban-ner of Je-sus entwined may it be, With our beau-ti-ful standard, "The Flag of the Free." The ban-ner of Je-sus, The ban-ner of Je-sus, The ban-ner of Je-sus, The Flag of the Free.

2. With the sword of the Spir-it, and pray'r for our shield, In the strength of the Lord let us on to the field; And the ban-ner of Je-sus shall wave o'er the sea, With our beau-ti-ful standard, "The Flag of the Free." The ban-ner, &c.

3 Lo! the angel of hope, from the portals of day,
Drops a smile like a sunbeam of joy on our way;
She will blend them in beauty, and wave o'er the sea,
With the banner of Jesus, "The Flag of the Free."—CHORUS.

3 Let us stand by the cross till our duty is done,
Till the conflict is o'er, and our victory is won;
Till our nation to Jesus united shall be,
And the banner of Jesus, "The Flag of the Free."—CHORUS.

JESUS WILL WELCOME ME.

T. E. P.

2. How sweet are the visions of rapture,
   Which often by faith I behold:
   The saints in their garments of beauty,
   A city where streets are of gold!—Cho.

3. Dear Saviour, I long to behold thee,
   I long in thy image to rise;
   Oh, when, like a bird on its pinions,
   Say, when shall I soar to the skies?—Cho.

THE JASPER SEA.

Words by JOSEPHINE POLLARD.   Music by W. H. DOANE.

2. With the angels round the throne,
   Robed in white, we'll stand ;
   Death and tears are never known
   In that happy land.—Cho.

3. Captive chains shall bind no more,
   When death sets us free,
   When we reach the other shore
   O'er the Jasper sea.—Cho.

4. Parting days will never come,
   Bright our lot will be,
   When we reach our heavenly home
   O'er the Jasper sea.—Cho.

5. To the judgment-seat above,
   Swiftly we repair,
   Saved from wrath through Jesus' love
   We shall see him there.—Cho.

98. JESUS MAKE ME FAITHFUL.

Words by Mrs. M. A. KIDDER.

1. There is a home in glo-ry, A bless-ed place of rest, Where I, if on-ly faith-ful, May dwell a-mong the blest.

Chorus.
Je-sus, make me faith-ful: An-gels pure and blest, Bear me on-ward, gent-ly on-ward, To that sweet home of rest.

2. There is a home of beauty,
It lies beyond the tomb,
Where darkness never enters,
Where flowers eternal bloom.
Cho.—Jesus make, etc.

3. Within that home celestial
No sorrow e'er can come,
No sin and no temptation—
O blissful, happy home!
Cho.—Jesus make, etc.

4. My earthly home is fading,
And heaven is just in sight:
Oh, bear me, blessed angels,
To mansions of delight.
Cho.—Jesus make, etc.

BETHANY.

Dr. L. MASON. By permission.

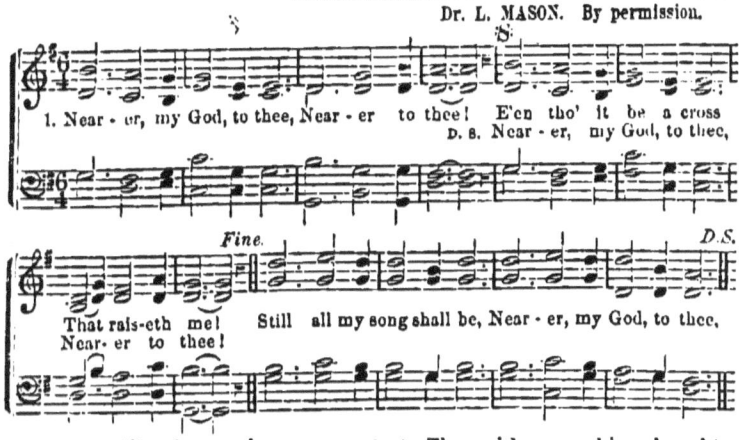

2. Though like the wanderer,
   The sun gone down,
   Darkness be over me,
   My rest a stone,
   Yet in my dreams I'd be,
   Nearer my God, to thee,
   Nearer to thee!

3. There let the way appear
   Steps unto heaven;
   All that thou sendest me,
   In mercy given;
   Angels to beckon me,
   Nearer, my God, to thee,
   Nearer to thee.

4. Then with my waking thoughts,
   Bright with thy praise,
   Out of my stony griefs
   Bethel I'll raise;
   So by my woes to be
   Nearer, my God, to thee,
   Nearer to thee!

5. Or if, on joyful wing,
   Cleaving the skies,
   Sun, moon and stars forgot,
   Upward I fly,
   Still all my song shall be,
   Nearer, my God, to thee,
   Nearer to thee.

ST. THOMAS. S. M.

2. Here on the mercy-seat,
   With radiant glory crowned,
   Our joyful eyes behold him sit,
   And smile on all around.

3. Give me, O Lord, a place
   Within thy blest abode,
   Among the children of thy grace,
   The servants of my God.

3 Kindly heaven smiles above,
　When there's love at home;
All the earth is filled with love,
　When there's love at home.
Sweeter sings the brooklet by,
Brighter beams the azure sky,
Oh, there's One who smiles on high
　When there's love at home.

4 Jesus, make me wholly thine,
　Then there's love at home;
May thy sacrifice be mine,
　Then there's love at home.
Safely from all harm I'll rest,
With no sinful care distressed,
Thro' thy tender mercy blessed
　With thy love at home.

HERE IS NO REST.

1. Here o'er the earth as a stranger I roam, Here is no rest, Here is no rest! Here as a pil-grim I wan-der a-lone, Yet I am blest, I am blest; For I look for-ward to that glorious day, When sin and sor-row shall van-ish a-way;
D.S. My heart doth leap while I hear Jesus say,
There, there is rest, there is rest.

2. Here are afflictions and trials severe,
  Here is no rest, here is no rest!
Here I must part with the friends I hold dear,
  Yet I am blest, I am blest!
Sweet is the promise I read in his word;
Blessed are those who have died in the Lord;
They have been called to receive their reward,
  There, there is rest, there is rest!

3. This world of care is a wilderness state,
  Here is no rest, here is no rest!
Here must I bear from the world all its hate,
  Yet I am blest, I am blest!
Soon shall I be from the wicked released,
Soon shall the weary forever be blest,
Soon shall I lean upon Jesus' own breast,
  There, there is rest, there is rest!

BEAUTIFUL RIVER.

Rev. R. LOWRY. By permission.

3. On the bosom of the river,
   Where the Saviour-king we own,
   We shall meet, and sorrow never,
   'Neath the glory of the throne.—Cho.

4. Ere we reach the shining river,
   Lay we every burden down;
   Grace our spirits will deliver,
   And provide a robe and crown.—Cho.

5. At the smiling of the river,
   Rippling with the Saviour's face,
   Saints, whom death will never sever,
   Lift their songs of saving grace.—Cho.

6. Soon we'll reach the shining river,
   Soon our pilgrimage will cease;
   Soon our happy hearts will quiver
   With the melody of peace.—Cho.

IVES. 7s.

E. IVES, Jr.

2 These through fiery trials trod;
  These from great affliction came;
Now, before the throne of God,
  Sealed with his almighty name:
Clad in raiment pure and white,
  Victor-palms in every hand,
Through their great Redeemer's might,
  More than conquerors they stand.

3 Hunger, thirst, disease, unknown,
  On immortal fruits they feed;
Them, the Lamb, amidst the throne,
  Shall to living fountains lead;
Joy and gladness banish sighs:
  Perfect love dispel all fears;
And forever from their eyes
  God shall wipe away their tears.

NEARER MY HOME.

1. A crown of glo-ry bright, By faith's clear eyes I see, In yonder realms of light, Prepared for me. I'm nearer my home,
2. Oh, may I faithful prove, And keep the crown in view, And through the storms of life My way pur-sue. I'm nearer, etc.

Chorus.

near-er my home, near-er my home to-day; Yes! near-er my home in heaven to-day Than ev-er I was be-fore.

Repeat very softly.

3 Jesus, be thou my guide,
My daily steps attend;
Oh, keep me near thy side,
Be thou my friend.—Cho.

4 Be thou my shield and sun,
My Saviour and my guard;
And when my work is done,
My great reward.—Cho.

AUTUMN. 8s & 7s. Double.

Spanish.

1. Glorious things of thee are spok-en, Zi-on, cit-y of our God!
He, whose word can-not be brok-en, Form'd thee for his own a-bode.
On the Rock of A-ges found-ed, What can shake thy sure re-pose?
With sal-va-tion's walls surround-ed, Thou may'st smile at all thy foes.

2. See! the streams of living waters
   Springing from eternal love;
  Well supply thy sons and daughters,
   And all fear of want remove.
  Who can faint while such a river
   Ever flows their thirst t' assunge;
  Grace which, like the Lord, the giver,
   Never fails from age to age?

3. Saviour, if of Zion's city
   I through grace a member am,
  Let the world deride or pity,
   I will glory in thy name.
  Fading is the worldling's pleasure,
   All his boasted pomp and show;
  Solid joys and lasting treasures,
   None but Zion's children know.

THE GOSPEL SHIP.

1. The gospel ship is sail-ing, sail-ing, sail-ing, The gospel ship is sail-ing,
All who would ship for glo-ry, glo-ry, glo-ry, All who would ship for glory,
Bound for Canaan's happy shore;
Come and welcome, rich and poor.
Glo-ry hal-le-lu-jah! All on board are sweet-ly sing-ing, Glo-ry hal-le-lu-jah! Hal-le-lu-jah to the Lamb.

2. She has landed many thousands, thousands, thousands,
She has landed many thousands
On fair Canaan's happy shore;
And thousands now are sailing, sailing, sailing,
And thousands now are sailing
Yet there's room for thousands more,
   Glory, hallelujah, &c.

3. Sails filled with heavenly breezes, breezes, breezes,
Sails filled with heavenly breezes,
Swiftly glides the ship along.
Her company are singing, singing, singing,
Her company are singing,
Glory, glory is their song.
   Glory, hallelujah, &c.

4. Take passage now for glory, glory, glory,
Take passage now for glory,
Sailing o'er life's troubled sea,
With us you shall be happy, happy, happy,
With us you shall be happy,
Happy through eternity.
   Glory, hallelujah, &c.

MARTYN. 7s.

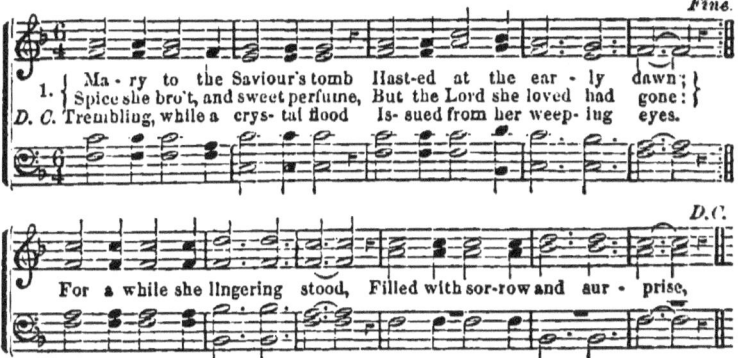

1. Ma-ry to the Saviour's tomb Hast-ed at the ear-ly dawn;
Spice she bro't, and sweet perfume, But the Lord she loved had gone:
D. C. Trembling, while a crys-tal flood Is-sued from her weep-ing eyes.
For a while she lingering stood, Filled with sor-row and sur-prise,

2. But her sorrows quickly fled
When she heard his welcome voice:
Christ has risen from the dead;
Now he bids her heart rejoice.
What a change his word can make,
Turning darkness into day;
Ye who weep for Jesus' sake,
He will wipe your tears away.

CHRIST THE ONLY REFUGE.

1. Jesus! lover of my soul,
Let me to thy bosom fly,
While the raging billows roll,
While the tempest still is high;
Hide me, O my Saviour! hide,
Till the storm of life is past;
Safe into the haven guide;
Oh, receive my soul at last!

2. Other refuge have I none,—
Hangs my helpless soul on thee!
Leave, ah! leave me not alone!
Still support and comfort me;
All my trust on thee is stayed;
All my help from thee I bring;
Cover my defenseless head
With the shadow of thy wing.

3. Thou, O Christ, art all I want;
All and all in thee I find;
Raise the fallen, cheer the faint,
Heal the sick, and lead the blind.
Just and holy is thy name,
I am all unrighteousness;
Vile, and full of sin I am,
Thou art full of truth and grace.

SWEETLY SING.

Words by Miss J. W. SAMPSON.

1. Sweet-ly sing, sweet-ly sing, Prais-es to our heavenly King;
Let us raise, Let us raise High our notes of praise:
Praise to Him whose name is Love, Praise to Him who reigns above;
Raise your songs, Raise your songs, Now with thank-ful tongues.

2.
Angels bright, angels bright,
Robed in garments pure and white,
Chant his praise, chant his praise,
In melodious lays:
But from that bright, happy throng,
Ne'er can come this sweetest song—
Redeeming love, redeeming love,
Brought us here above.

3.
Far away, far away,
We in sin's dark valley lay,
Jesus came, Jesus came,
Blessed be his name!
He redeemed us by his grace,
Then prepared in heaven a place
To receive—to receive
All who will believe.

4.
Now we know—now we know
We to heaven must shortly go,
Soon the call—soon the call
Comes to one and all.
Saviour! when *our* time shall come,
Take us to our heavenly home,
There we'll raise notes of praise,
Through unending days.

PASSING AWAY.

1. To-day, if you will hear his voice, Now is the time to make your choice;
Say, will you to Mount Zi-on go? Say, will you have this Christ, or no?
We are pass-ing a-way, We are pass-ing a-way, We are pass-ing a-way To the great Judgment-day.

2 Ye wandering souls, who find no rest,
Say, will you be forever blest?
Will you be saved from sin and hell?
Will you with Christ in glory dwell?—We are passing, &c.

3 Come now, dear friends, for ruin bound,
Obey the Gospel's joyful sound;
Come, go with us, and you shall prove
The joy of Christ's redeeming love.—We are passing, &c.

4 Leave all your sports and glittering toys;
Come, share with us eternal joys;
Or, must we leave you bound to hell?
Then, dearest friends, a long farewell.—We are passing, &c.

5 Once more, we ask you, in his name,
For yet his love remains the same :
Say, will you to Mount Zion go?
Say, will you have this Christ, or no?—We are passing, &c.

REST FOR THE WEARY.

Rev. J. W. DADMUN. By permission.

1. In the Christian's home in glo-ry, There remains a land of rest;
There my Saviour's gone be-fore me, To ful-fil my soul's re-quest.

Chorus.

{ There is rest for the wea-ry, There is rest for the wea-ry,
  On the oth-er side of Jor-dan, In the sweet fields of E-den,
  There is rest for the wea-ry, There is rest for you.
  Where the tree of life is blooming, There is rest for you. }

2. He is fitting up my mansion,
   Which eternally shall stand;
   For my stay shall not be transient,
   In that holy, happy land.—Cho.

3. Pain nor sickness ne'er shall enter,
   Grief nor woe my lot shall share;
   But in that celestial centre,
   I a crown of life shall wear.—Cho.

4. Death itself shall then be vanquished,
   And his sting shall be withdrawn;
   Shout for gladness, O ye ransomed!
   Hail with joy the rising morn.—Cho.

5. Sing, oh sing, ye heirs of glory!
   Shout your triumph as you go!
   Zion's gate will open for you,
   You shall find an entrance through.—Cho.

THE HAPPY LAND.

There is a hap-py land, Far, far a-way, Where saints in glory stand, Bright, bright as day. Oh, how they sweetly sing, Worthy is our Saviour King, Loud let his praises ring, Praise, praise for aye.

2. Come to that happy land,
   Come, come away;
   Why will ye doubting stand,
   Why still delay?
   Oh, we shall happy be,
   When from sin and sorrow free!
   Lord, we shall live with thee,
   Blest, blest for aye.

3. Bright, in that happy land,
   Beams every eye;
   Kept by a Father's hand
   Love cannot die.
   Oh, then to glory run,
   Be a crown and kingdom won;
   And, bright above the sun,
   We reign for aye.

PETERBOROUGH. C. M.

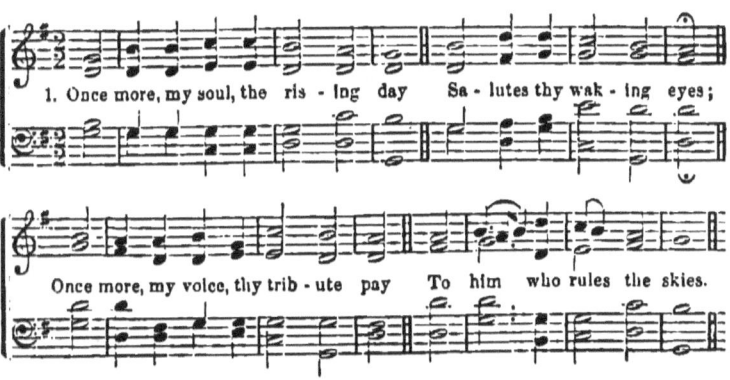

1. Once more, my soul, the ris-ing day Sa-lutes thy wak-ing eyes; Once more, my voice, thy trib-ute pay To him who rules the skies.

2. Night unto night his name repeats,
   The day renews the sound;
   Wide as the heaven, on which he sits,
   To turn the seasons round.

3. 'Tis he supports my mortal frame,
   My tongue shall speak his praise;
   My sins would rouse his wrath to flame,
   And yet his wrath delays.

3. Beautiful crowns on every brow.
Beautiful palms the conquerors show,
Beautiful robes the ransomed wear,
Beautiful all who enter there ;
Thither I press with eager feet.
There shall my rest be long and sweet.

4. Beautiful throne for Christ our King,
Beautiful songs the angels sing ;
Beautiful rest—all wanderings cease,
Beautiful home of perfect peace ;
There shall my eyes the Saviour see.
Haste to his heavenly home with me.

CHILDREN'S PRAISE.

1. Here we throng to praise the Lord, List-en now, List-en now,
Here we throng to praise the Lord With our in-fant lays.
He who once lay in a manger, Now enthroned, our blest Redeemer,
With a Fa-ther's love has said, He'd ac-cept our praise.

2. "Let young children come to me," Je-sus said, Je-sus said;
"Let young children come to me, And for-bid them not."
"For of such," the Saviour told them, "Is composed my heavenly king-[dom."]
What a rapturous thought it is, Christ for-gets us not!

3. Let us love, and now adore;
Love him now, love him now.
Let us love, and now adore,
In our youthful strength.
Let us never grieve our Saviour,
Who hath died to win us favor,
Ah! this thought should melt our hearts—
Children's hearts can melt.

4. But we'll have a joyous song,
Joyous song, joyous song;
But we'll have a joyous song
For our jubilee.
Jesus lives and reigns forever:
This will make us joyous ever.
Saviour, hear this praise to thee,
Who remembered me.

114 — TO BE LIKE JESUS.

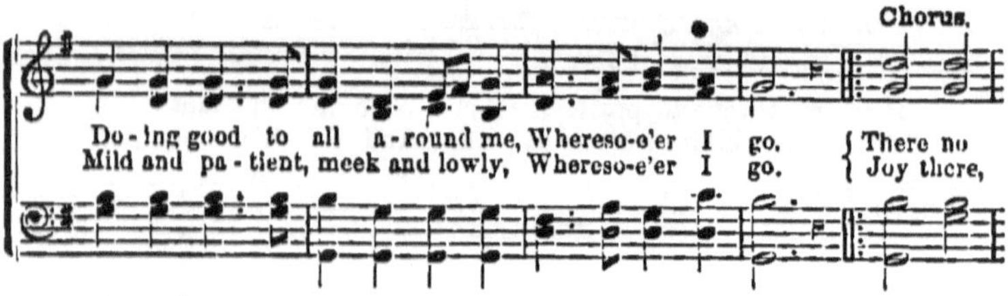

1. How I long to be like Jesus, How I long to be like Jesus,
2. How I long to be like Jesus, How I long to be like Jesus,

Doing good to all a-round me, Whereso-e'er I go.
Mild and pa-tient, meek and lowly, Whereso-e'er I go.

Chorus.

There no Joy there,

|1st.| more to sev-er, Dwell with him for ev-er; like a riv-er, [Omit............ ....] |2d.| Shall for-ev-er flow.

3. How I long to be like Jesus,
   How I long to be like Jesus,
   Kind, forgiving those who wrong me,
   Wheresoe'er I go.—Cho.

4. How I long to be like Jesus,
   How I long to be like Jesus,
   Like my Saviour, pure and holy,
   Wheresoe'er I go.—Cho.

THE SWEETEST NAME.

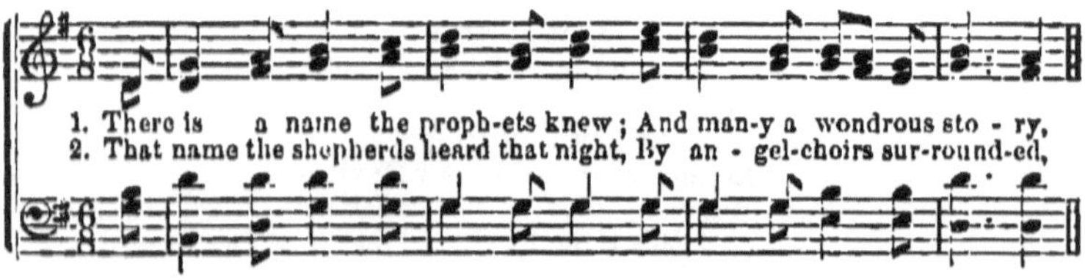

1. There is a name the proph-ets knew; And man-y a wondrous sto-ry,
2. That name the shepherds heard that night, By an- gel-choirs sur-round-ed,

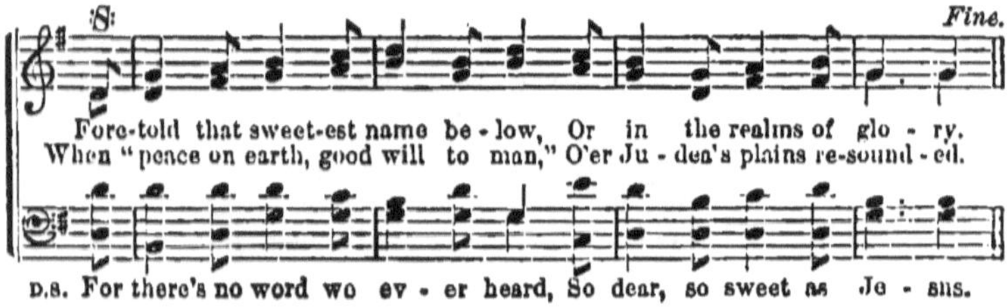

Fine.

Fore-told that sweet-est name be-low, Or in the realms of glo-ry.
When "peace on earth, good will to man," O'er Ju-dea's plains re-sound-ed.

D.S. For there's no word we ev-er heard, So dear, so sweet as Je-sus.

THE SWEETEST NAME.

3. In every prayer for strength divine,
In every time of sadness,
That name we plead, that name we praise,
It fills our hearts with gladness.

4. Dear name! the anchor of the soul,
The only source of pleasure,
The spring of hope, the fount of life,
Our best, our purest treasure.

LITTLE THINGS.

Words by Miss FANNY CROSBY.   From "New Shining Star."

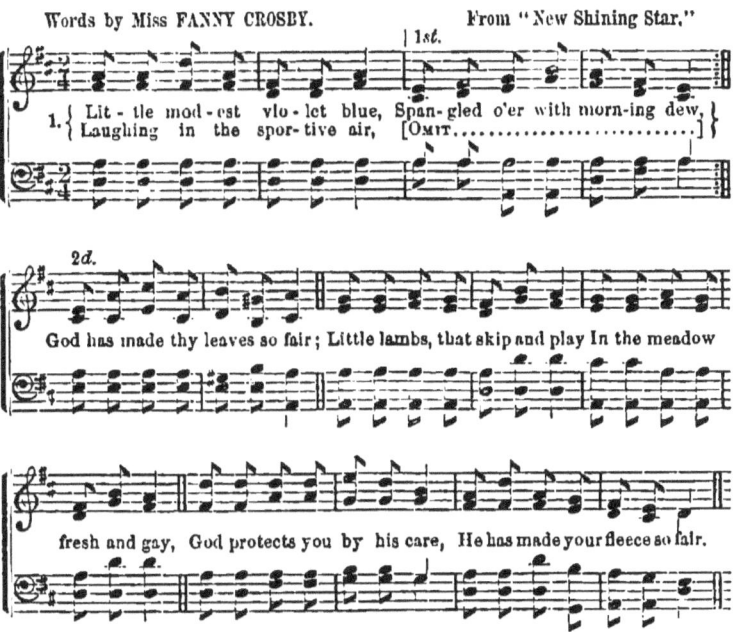

2. Little star with golden eye,
God has placed thee in the sky;
Little bird with glassy wing,
God has taught thee how to sing;
Little clouds, that lightly rest
On the bosom of the west,
Floating in the summer air,
God has made your form so fair.

3. Little merry, laughing child,
Ever playful, ever wild,
Full of gladness, full of love,
God has made thee, God above;
He thy little spirit keeps,
For he never, never sleeps;
When thy little life is past
He will take thee home at last.

HOME. 11s.

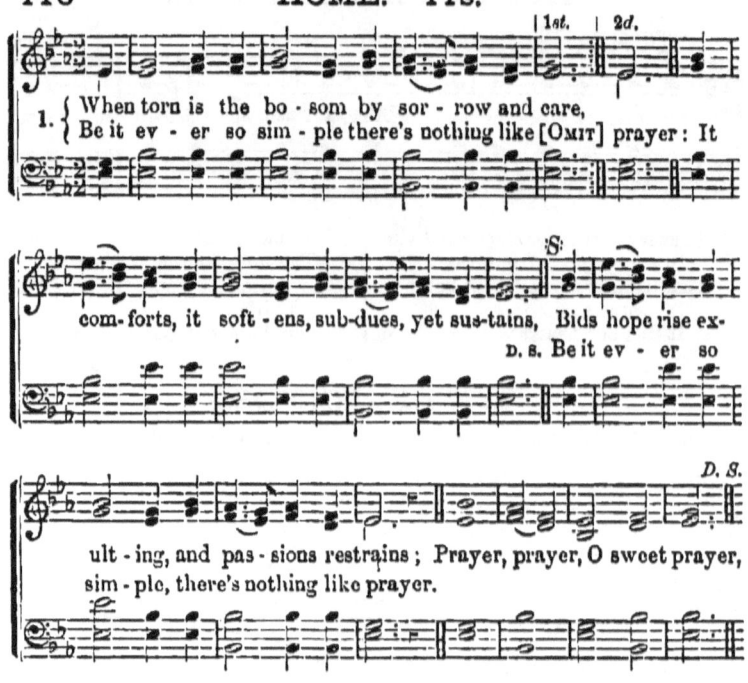

1. When torn is the bosom by sorrow and care,
   Be it ever so simple there's nothing like [Omit] prayer: It comforts, it softens, subdues, yet sustains, Bids hope rise exulting, and passions restrains; Prayer, prayer, O sweet prayer, Be it ever so simple, there's nothing like prayer.

2. When far from the friends that are dearest we part,
   What fond recollections still cling to the heart;
   Past scenes and enjoyment live painfully there;
   And restless we languish, till peace comes in prayer. Prayer, &c.

3. When earthly delusions would lead us astray
   In folly's gay mazes, or sin's treacherous way,
   How strong the enchantment, how fatal the snare!
   But looking to Jesus, we conquer by prayer. Prayer, &c.

4. While strangers to prayer, we are strangers to bliss,
   The world has no refuge, no solace like this;
   And till we the seraph's full ecstacy share,
   Our chalice of joy must be guarded by prayer. Prayer, &c.

GLORY IN THE HIGHEST.

Words by FANNY CROSBY.   Music by T. E. PERKINS.

1. Merry, merry chiming bells, Stealing o'er the silent dells, Happy

GLORY IN THE HIGHEST. 117

news their music tells, Glo-ry in the High-est, Glo-ry in the High-est.

2. In a manger far away,
Once the infant Saviour lay,
He was born on Christmas-day,
Glory in the Highest.

3. Born to die for you and me,
Born to set the captive free;
Prophets longed his birth to see,
Glory in the Highest.

4. With the bells that sweetly chime,
Soon shall every heathen clime
Hail the happy Christmas time,
Glory in the Highest.

5. Let the joyful echo fly,
Angels sing and earth reply,
Glory be to God on high,
Glory in the Highest.

FREDERICK. 11s. GEO. KINGSLEY.

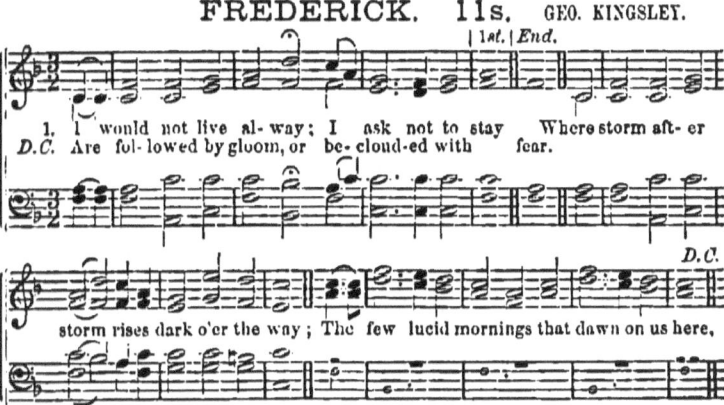

1. I would not live al-way; I ask not to stay Where storm aft-er
D.C. Are fol-lowed by gloom, or be-cloud-ed with fear.

storm rises dark o'er the way; The few lucid mornings that dawn on us here,

2. I would not live alway thus fettered by sin—
Temptation without and corruption within;
E'en the rapture of pardon is mingled with fears,
And the cup of thanksgiving with penitent tears.

4. I would not live alway; no—welcome the tomb;
Since Jesus hath lain there I dread not its gloom;
There sweet be my rest till he bid me arise
To hail him in triumph descending the skies.

4. Who, who would live alway away from his God—
Away from yon heaven, that blissful abode,
Where rivers of pleasure flow bright o'er the plains,
And the noontide of glory eternally reigns?

5. There saints of all ages in harmony meet,
There Saviour and brethren transported to greet,
While anthems of rapture unceasingly roll,
And the smile of the Lord is the feast of the soul.

SHINING SHORE.

GEORGE F. ROOT. By permission.

1. My days are glid-ing swift-ly by, And I, a pil-grim stran-ger, Would not de-tain them as they fly,—Those hours of toil and dan-ger. For now we stand on Jor-dan's strand, Our friends are pass-ing o-ver; And

D. S. just be-fore the shin-ing shore, We may al-most dis-cov-er.

2. We'll gird our loins, my brother dear,
   Our heavenly home discerning;
   Our absent Lord has left us word,
   Let every lamp be burning.
   For now we stand, &c.

3. Should coming days be cold and dark,
   We need not cease our singing;
   That perfect rest naught can molest
   Where golden harps are ringing.
   For now we stand, &c.

4. Let sorrow's rudest tempest blow,
   Each chord on earth to sever,
   Our King says come, and there's our home,
   Forever! oh, forever!
   For now we stand, &c.

CROSS AND CROWN. 119

3. The consecrated cross I'll bear,
   Till death shall set me free,
   And then go home, my crown to wear—
   For there's a crown for me.

DUKE STREET. L. M.

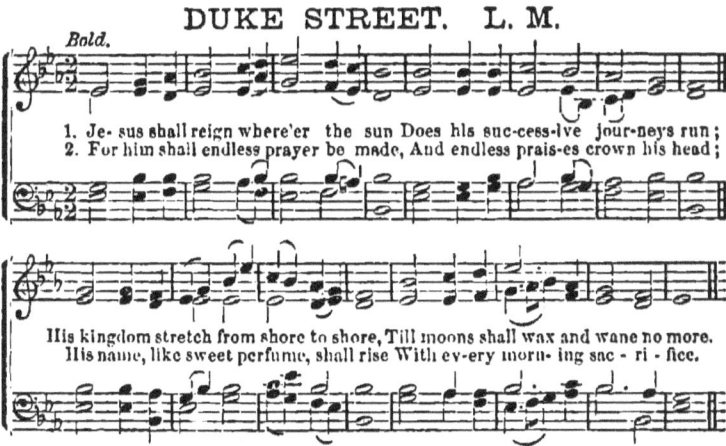

3. People and realms of every tongue
   Dwell on his love, with sweetest song;
   And infant voices shall proclaim
   Their early blessings on his name.

4. Blessings abound where'er he reigns:
   The pris'ner leaps to lose his chains;
   The weary find eternal rest,
   And all the sons of want are blest.

5. Let every creature rise and bring
   Peculiar honors to our King:
   Angels descend with songs again,
   And earth repeat the loud Amen.

120 WORK, FOR THE NIGHT IS COMING.

From "Song Garden," by permission of MASON BROTHERS.

1. Work, for the night is com-ing, Work thro' the morning hours;
Work, while the dew is spark-ling, Work 'mid springing flow'rs;
Work when the day grows brighter, Work in the glowing sun;
Work, for the night is com'- ing, When man's work is done.

2. Work for the night is coming,
Work thro' the sunny noon;
Fill brightest hours with labor,
Rest comes sure and soon.
Give every flying minute,
Something to keep in store:
Work, for the night is coming,
When man works no more.

3. Work, for the night is coming,
Under the sunset skies;
While their bright tints are glowing
Work, for daylight flies.
Work till the last beam fadeth,
Fadeth to shine no more;
Work while the night is dark'ning,
When man's work is o'er.

BARTIMEUS. 8s & 7s. 121

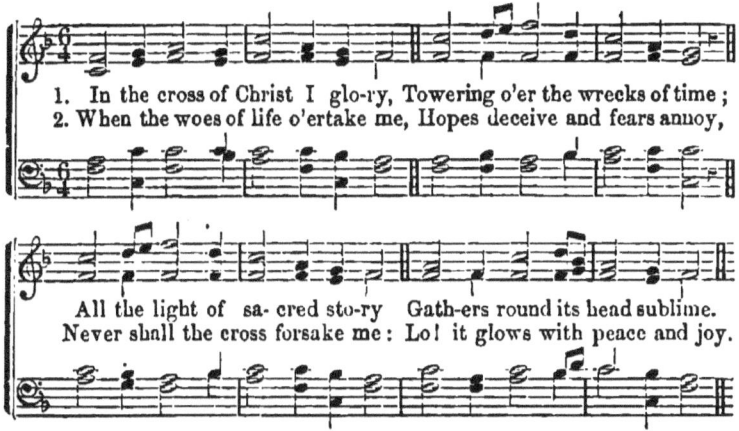

1. In the cross of Christ I glo-ry, Towering o'er the wrecks of time;
2. When the woes of life o'ertake me, Hopes deceive and fears annoy,

All the light of sa-cred sto-ry Gath-ers round its head sublime.
Never shall the cross forsake me: Lo! it glows with peace and joy.

3. When the sun of bliss is beaming
   Light and love upon my way,
   From the cross the radiance streaming
   Adds new lustre to the day.

4. Bane and blessing, pain and pleasure,
   By the cross are sanctified ;
   Peace is there that knows no measure,
   Joys that through all time abide.

5. In the cross of Christ I glory,
   Towering o'er the wrecks of time;
   All the light of sacred story
   Gathers round its head sublime.

I WAS GLAD WHEN THEY SAID.

Dr. L. MASON. By permission.

1. I was glad when they said unto me, let us go into the | house·· of the | Lord.
2. Our feet shall stand within thy gates, O Jerusalem; Jerusalem is builded as a city that | is com- | pact to- | gether.
3. Whither the tribes go up: the tribes of the Lord, unto the testimony of Israel, to give thanks unto the | name·· of the | Lord.
4. For there are set thrones of judgment, the | thrones·· of the | house of | David.
5. Pray for the peace of Jerusalem, they shall | prosper··that [thee. love
6. Peace be within thy walls; and pros- | peri-ty with- | in thy | palaces.
7. For my brethren and companion's sakes, I will now say, | Peace··be with- | in thee. [A- | men.
8. Because of the house of the Lord our God, I will | seek thy | good.

MARCHING SONG. 123

fail, For our Cap-tain we will no-bly fight, and in his strength prevail.

3. Who will join our army? though the struggle may be long,
   Nobly we will brave it, for our hearts in God are strong;
   If we trust our great Commander, aid and comfort we shall find,
   And he'll drive the foe before us, like the chaff before the wind.

4. Onward, ever onward, then our steady course we'll keep,
   Onward, ever onward, till we climb the mountain steep:
   For our Captain's gone before us, and the war will soon be past,
   He has promised all his faithful ones a glorious crown at last.

O HEAVEN, DEAR HEAVEN.

1. How hap-py ev-ery child of grace, Who knows his sins for-given!
   This earth, he cries, is not my place, I seek my place in heaven;
   D. C. To dwell for-ev-er with the blest, E-ter-nal joys to share.

Chorus.
O heaven, dear heaven, sweet land of rest, When shall my soul be there,

2. A country far from mortal sight,
   Yet, oh, by faith I see
   The land of rest, the saints' delight—
   The heaven prepared for me.—CHORUS.

3. Oh, what a blessed hope is ours
   While here on earth we stay,
   We more than taste the heavenly powers,
   And ante-date that day.—CHORUS.

4. We feel the resurrection near,—
   Our life in Christ conceal'd,
   And with his glorious presence here
   Our earthen vessels fill'd.—CHORUS.

MERCY'S FREE.

From "The Silver Fountain." By permission of A. J. ABBEY.

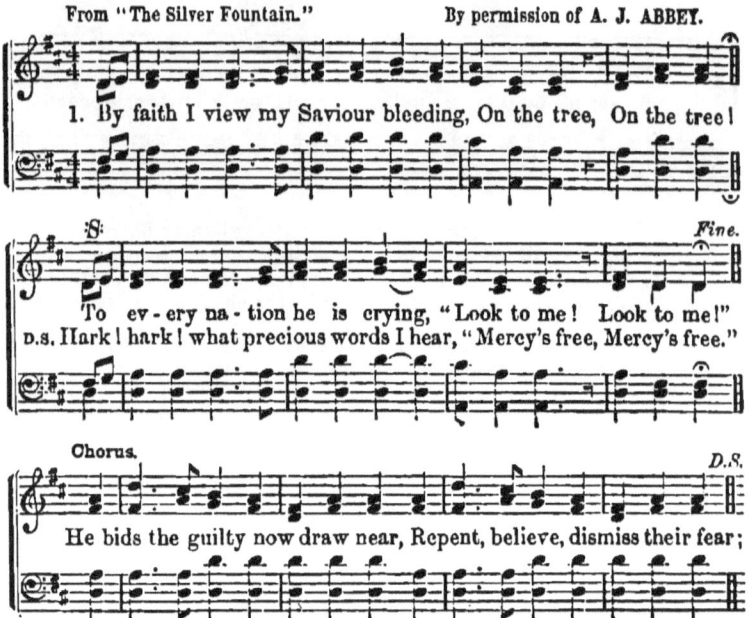

1. By faith I view my Saviour bleeding, On the tree, On the tree!
To ev-ery na-tion he is crying, "Look to me! Look to me!"
D.S. Hark! hark! what precious words I hear, "Mercy's free, Mercy's free."

Chorus.
He bids the guilty now draw near, Repent, believe, dismiss their fear;

2. Did Christ, when I was sin pursuing,
   Pity me?
And did he snatch my soul from ruin,—
   Can it be?
Oh yes, he did salvation bring;
He is my Prophet, Priest, and King;
And now my happy soul can sing,
   "Mercy's free!"

3. Jesus, my weary soul refreshes,
   Mercy's free!
And every moment Christ is precious
   Unto me.
None can describe the bliss I prove,
While through this wilderness I rove;
All may enjoy the Saviour's love;
   Mercy's free!

4. Long as I live, I'll still be crying,
   "Mercy's free!"
And this shall be my theme when dying,
   "Mercy's free!"
And when the vale of death I've passed,
When safe beyond the stormy blast,
I'll sing while endless ages last,
   "Mercy's free!"

JESUS, MY ALL.

1. Lord, at thy mercy-seat, Humbly I fall;
Pleading thy promise sweet, Lord, hear my call;
Now let thy work begin, Oh, make me pure within,
Cleanse me from every sin, Jesus, my all.

2. Tears of repentant grief
Silently fall;
Help thou my unbelief,
Hear thou my call.
Oh, how I pine for thee!
'Tis all my hope, my plea:
Jesus has died for me;
Jesus, my all.

3. Hark! how the words of love
Tenderly fall,
Ere to the realms above,
Heard is my call;
Now every doubt has flown,
Broken my heart of stone,
Lord, I am thine alone,
Jesus, my all.

4. Still at thy mercy-seat
Humbly I fall;
Pleading thy promise sweet,
Heard is my call.
Faith wings my soul to thee,
This all my hope shall be,
Jesus has died for me,
Jesus, my all.

JESUS, I LONG FOR THEE.

1. Jesus, I long for thee,
Friendless I roam;
Earth has no joy for me,
Heaven is my home;
When shall my soul arise,
Joyful with glad surprise,
Up to its native skies?
Heaven is my home.

2. Grant me a light divine,
While here I roam,
O'er my dark path to shine,
Heaven is my home.
Oh, my sad heart, be still
Patient in every ill,
Thine be a Father's will;
Heaven is my home.

3. There shall I see his face,
No more to roam;
Clasped in his dear embrace;
Heaven is my home.
Soon shall my spirit rise,
Joyful with glad surprise,
Up to its native skies;
Heaven is my home.

SHOUT THE GLAD TIDINGS. 127

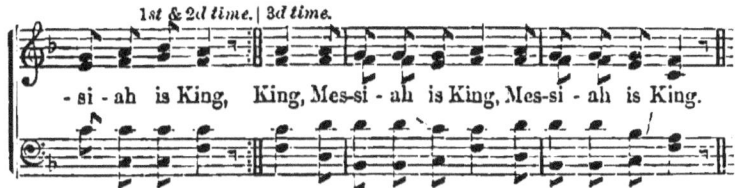

2. Tell how he cometh from nation to nation,
The heart-cheering news let the earth echo round;
How free to the faithful he offers salvation,
How his people with joy everlasting are crown'd. Shout, &c.

3. Mortals, your homage be gratefully bringing,
And sweet let the gladsome hosanna arise:
Ye angels, the full hallelujah be singing;
One chorus resound thro' the earth and the skies. Shout, &c.

THE GOLDEN RULE.

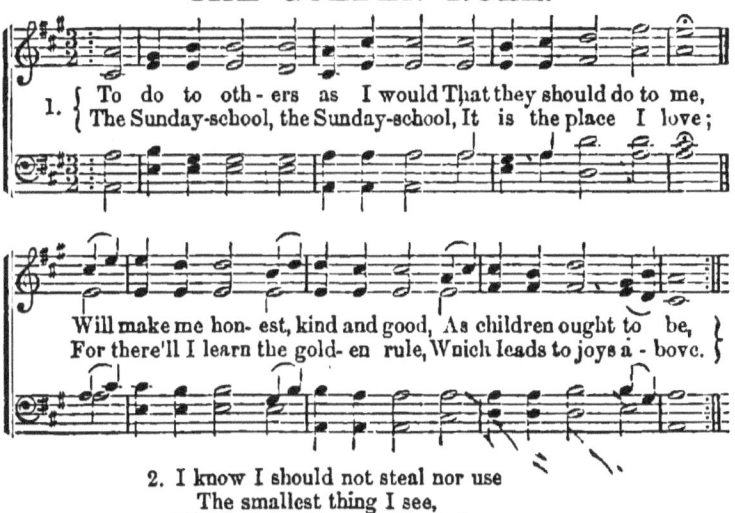

2. I know I should not steal nor use
The smallest thing I see,
Which I should never like to lose
If it belonged to me. The Sunday-school, &c.

3. And this plain rule forbids me quite
To strike an angry blow,
Because I should not think it right
If others served me so. The Sunday-school, &c.

4. But any kindness they may need
I'll do whate'er it be:
As I am very glad indeed
When they are kind to me. The Sunday-school, &c.

ROCK OF AGES.

Dr. T. HASTINGS.

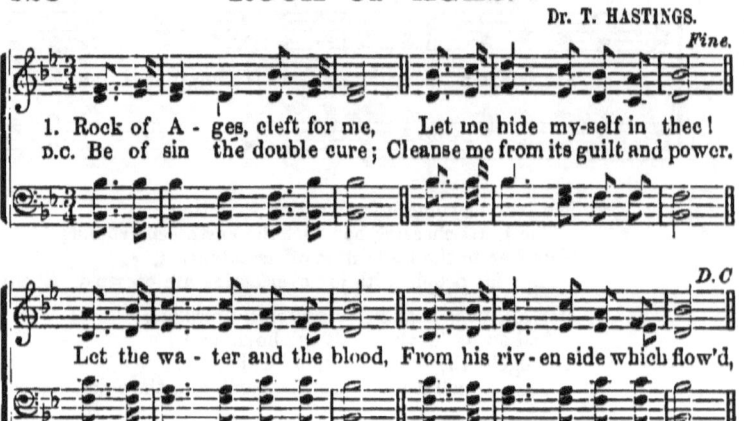

1. Rock of A - ges, cleft for me, Let me hide my-self in thee!
D.C. Be of sin the double cure; Cleanse me from its guilt and power.

Let the wa - ter and the blood, From his riv - en side which flow'd,

2. Not the labors of my hands
Can fulfil the law's demands:
Could my zeal no respite know,
Could my tears forever flow,
All for sin could not atone;
Thou must save, and thou alone!

3. Nothing in my hand I bring;
Simply to thy cross I cling;
Naked, come to thee for dress;

Helpless, look to thee for grace;
Foul, I to thy fountain fly;
Wash me, Saviour, or I die!

4. While I draw this fleeting breath,
When my eyestrings break in death,
When I soar to worlds unknown,
See thee on thy judgment throne
Rock of Ages, cleft for me,
Let me hide myself in thee.

HOMEWARD BOUND.

Rev. J. W. DADMUN. By permission.

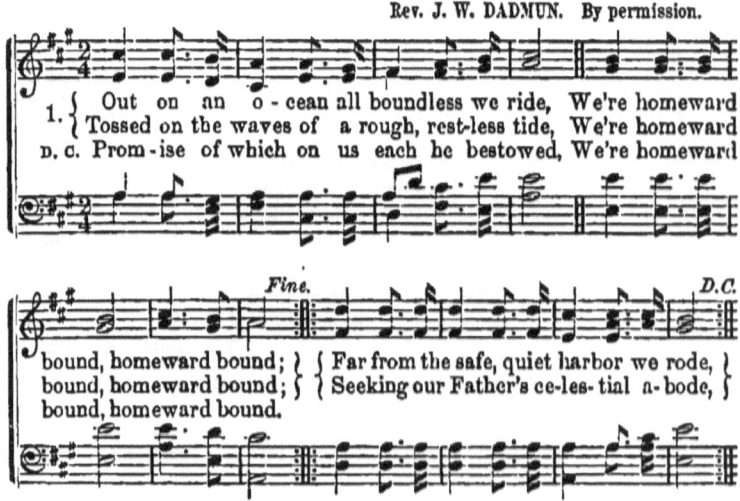

1. { Out on an o - cean all boundless we ride, We're homeward
{ Tossed on the waves of a rough, rest-less tide, We're homeward
D.C. Prom-ise of which on us each he bestowed, We're homeward

bound, homeward bound; } { Far from the safe, quiet harbor we rode,
bound, homeward bound; } { Seeking our Father's ce-les-tial a-bode,
bound, homeward bound.

HOMEWARD BOUND. 129

2. Wildly the storm sweeps us on as it roars; We're homeward bound;
Look! yonder lie the bright heavenly shores, We're homeward bound;
Steady, O pilot! stand firm at the wheel;
Steady! we soon shall outweather the gale;
Oh, how we fly 'neath the loud creaking sail!
We're homeward bound.

3. We'll tell the world, as we journey along, We're homeward bound;
Try to persuade them to enter our throng, We're homeward bound;
Come, trembling sinner, forlorn and oppressed,
Join in our number, oh come, and be blest;
Journey with us to the mansions of rest;
We're homeward bound.

4. Into the harbor of heaven we now glide; We're home at last;
Softly we drift on its bright silver tide; We're home at last;
Glory to God! all our dangers are o'er;
We stand secure on the glorified shore;
Glory to God! we will shout evermore;
We're home at last

MOUNT PISGAH. C. M.

1. Am I a soldier of the cross, A follower of the Lamb?
And shall I fear to own his cause, Or blush to speak his name

Chorus.
Or blush to speak his name? Or blush to speak his name?

2. Must I be carried to the skies
On flowery beds of ease,
While others fought to win the prize,
Or sailed through bloody seas?

3. Are there no foes for me to face?
Must I not stem the flood?
Is this vile world a friend to grace,
To help me on to God?

130. MISSIONARY HYMN. 7s & 6s.
Dr. LOWELL MASON.

1. From Greenland's i-cy mountains, From In-dia's cor-al strand,
Where Af-ric's sun-ny foun-tains Roll down their gold-en sand;
From many an an-cient riv-er, From many a palm-y plain,
They call us to de-liv-er Their land from er-ror's chain.

2. What tho' the spi-cy breez-es Blow soft o'er Cey-lon's isle,
Though ev-ery prospect pleas-es, And on-ly man is vile;
In vain with lav-ish kind-ness The gifts of God are strown,
The hea-then, in his blindness, Bows down to wood and stone.

3. Can we whose souls are lighted
By wisdom from on high,
Can we to men benighted
The lamp of light deny?
Salvation, O salvation!
The joyful sound proclaim,
Till earth's remotest nation
Has learned Messiah's name.

4. Waft, waft, ye winds, his story,
And you, ye waters, roll,
Till, like a sea of glory,
It spreads from pole to pole:
Till o'er our ransomed nature,
The Lamb for sinners slain,
Redeemer, King, Creator,
In bliss returns to reign.

NO SORROW THERE.

Where many a friend is gathered safe, From fear, and toil, and care.
In heaven a-bove, where all is love, There'll be no sor-row there.

2. I love to think of heaven,
    Where my Redeemer reigns;
    Where rapturous songs of triumph rise
    In endless, joyous strains.—Cho.

3. I love to think of heaven,
    The saints' eternal home;
    Where palms, and robes, and crowns ne'er fade,
    And all our joys are one.—Cho.

4. I love to think of heaven,
    The greetings there we'll meet:
    The harps—the songs for ever ours—
    The walks—the golden streets.—Cho.

5. I love to think of heaven,
    That promised land so fair,
    Oh, how my raptured spirit longs
    To be for ever there.—Cho.

SWEET LAND OF REST.

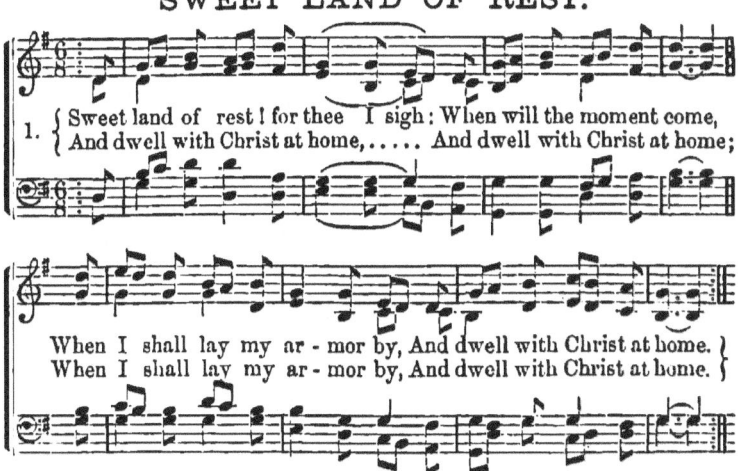

1. { Sweet land of rest! for thee I sigh: When will the moment come,
    And dwell with Christ at home,..... And dwell with Christ at home;
    When I shall lay my ar-mor by, And dwell with Christ at home.
    When I shall lay my ar-mor by, And dwell with Christ at home.

2. No tranquil joys on earth I know,
    No peaceful sheltering home;
    This world's a wilderness of woe,
    This world is not my home.

3. To Jesus Christ I sought for rest,
    He bade me cease to roam,
    But fly for succor to his breast,
    And he'd conduct me home.

I LOVE JESUS.

Arranged by T. E. PERKINS.

2. Teach me some melodious sonnet,
   Sung by flaming tongues above;
   Praise the mount—oh, fix me on it
   Mount of God's unchanging love.

3. Here I raise my Ebenezer;
   Hither, by thy help I'm come;
   And I hope, by thy good pleasure,
   Safely to arrive at home.

I'M A PILGRIM.

I'M A PILGRIM.

2. There the glory is ever shining;
I am longing, I am longing for the sight;
Here in this country, so dark and dreary,
I have been wand'ring forlorn and weary.
I'm a pilgrim, and I'm a stranger;
I can tarry, I can tarry but a night.

3. There's the city to which I journey;
My Redeemer, my Redeemer is its light;
There is no sorrow, nor any sighing,
There is no sin there, nor any dying.
I'm a pilgrim, and I'm a stranger;
I can tarry, I can tarry but a night.

JOYFULLY. Rev. WM. HUNTER.

1. Joy-ful-ly, joy-ful-ly on-ward I move, Bound to the land of bright
An-gel-ic chor-is-ters sing as I come, Joy-ful-ly, joy-ful-ly
spir-its above; Soon with my pilgrimage ended be-low,
haste to thy home! Home to the land of bright spirits I go; Pil-grim and
stran-ger no more shall I roam, Joy-ful-ly, joy-ful-ly rest-ing at home.

2. Friends, fondly cherished, have passed on before;
Waiting, they watch me approaching the shore;
Singing to cheer me through death's chilling gloom,
Joyfully, joyfully, haste to thy home.
Sounds of sweet melody fall on my ear;
Harps of the blessed, your voices I hear
Rings with the harmony heaven's high dome,—
Joyfully, joyfully haste to thy home.

3. Death, with thy weapons of war lay me low;
Strike, king of terrors, I fear not the blow;
Jesus hath broken the bars of the tomb!
Joyfully, joyfully will I go home.
Bright will the morn of eternity dawn,
Death shall be banished, his sceptre be gone,—
Joyfully, then, shall I witness his doom,
Joyfully, joyfully, safely at home

A LOVER OF THE LORD.

2. Return, O wand'rer, to thy home,
   'Tis Jesus calls for thee;
   The Spirit and the Bride say, come;
   Oh! now for refuge flee. —Cho.

3. Return, O wand'rer, to thy home,
   'Tis madness to delay;
   There are no pardons in the tomb,
   And brief is mercy's day.—Cho.

GOING HOME.

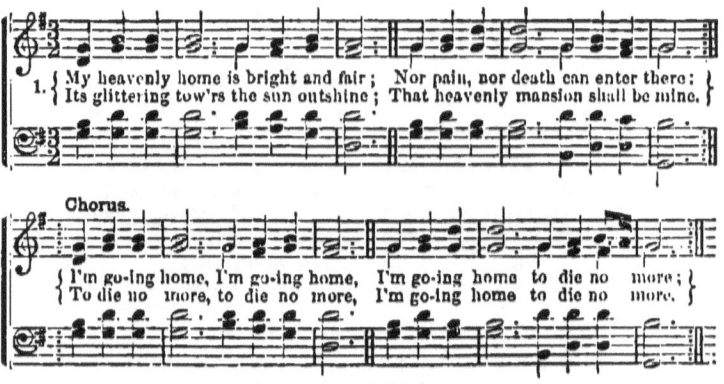

2. My Father's house is built on high,
   Far, far above the starry sky;
   When from this earthly prison free,
   That heavenly mansion mine shall be.—Cho.

GOING HOME. 139

3. Let others seek a home below,
Which flames devour, or waves o'erflow;
Be mine a happier lot to own,
A heavenly mansion near the throne.—Cho.

COME TO JESUS JUST NOW.

REV. EDWARD PAYSON HAMMOND *says this was first sung in Scotland, when hundreds were asking, "What shall we do to be saved?"*

With feeling and earnestness.

1. Come to Je-sus, come to Je-sus, Come to Je-sus just now, just now; Come to Je-sus, come to Je-sus, just now.

SUPT.—"COME UNTO ME, all ye that labor and are heavy laden, and I will give you rest."—Matt. xi. 28.

1. *Come to Jesus, just now*, etc.

SUPT.—"Believe on the Lord Jesus Christ, and thou shalt be SAVED."—Acts xvi. 31.

2. *He will save you, just now*, etc.

SUPT.—"God so loved the world that he gave his only-begotten Son, that whosoever BELIEVETH in him should not perish, but have everlasting life."—John iii. 16.

3. *Oh, believe him, just now*, etc.

SUPT.—"He is ABLE to save them to the uttermost that come unto God by him, seeing he ever liveth to make intercession for us."—Heb. vii. 25.

4. *He is able, just now*, etc.

SUPT.—"The Lord is long-suffering to usward, not WILLING that any should perish, but that all should come to repentance."—2 Pet. iii. 9.

5. *He is willing, just now*, etc.

SUPT.—"Him that cometh to me, I WILL IN NO WISE CAST OUT."—John vi. 37.

6. *He'll receive you, just now*, etc.

SUPT.—"FLEE from the wrath to come."—Matt. iii. 7.

7. *Flee to Jesus, just now*, etc.

SUPT.—"Whosoever shall CALL on the name of the Lord shall be saved."—Acts ii. 21.

8. *Call unto him, just now*, etc.

SUPT.—"And Jesus said unto him, Go thy way; THY FAITH HATH MADE THEE WHOLE."—Mark x. 25.

9. *He will hear you, just now*, etc.

SUPT.—"Jesus, thou son of David, have MERCY on me."—Mark x. 47.

10. *He'll have mercy, just now*, etc.

SUPT.—"If we confess our sins, he is faithful and just to FORGIVE US our sins.—1 John i. 9.

11. *He'll forgive you, just now*, etc.

SUPT.—"The blood of Jesus Christ, his Son CLEANSETH US from all sin."—1 John i. 7.

12. *He will cleanse you, just now*, etc.

SUPT.—"Therefore, if any man be in Christ, he is a NEW CREATURE."—2 Cor. v. 17.

13. *He'll renew you, just now*, etc.

SUPT.—"He that overcometh, the same shall be CLOTHED in white raiment."—Rev. iii. 5.

14. *He will clothe you, just now*, etc.

SUPT.—"Greater LOVE hath no man than this, that a man should lay down his life for his friends."—John xv. 13.

15. *Jesus loves you, just now*, etc.

AMERICA. 6s & 4s.

Words by F. SMITH.

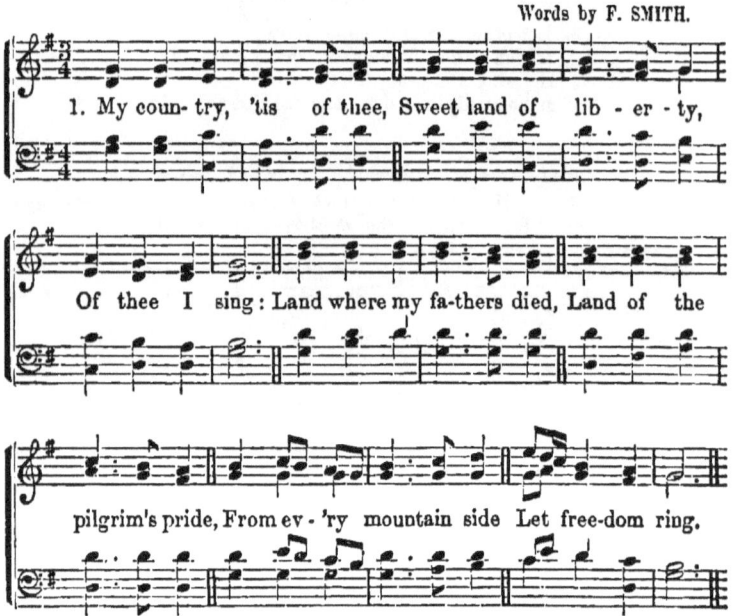

1. My country, 'tis of thee, Sweet land of liberty, Of thee I sing: Land where my fathers died, Land of the pilgrim's pride, From ev-'ry mountain side Let freedom ring.

2.
My native country, thee—
Land of the noble, free—
 Thy name I love;
I love thy rocks and rills,
Thy woods and templed hills;
My heart with rapture thrills
 Like that above.

3.
Let music swell the breeze,
And ring from all the trees
 Sweet freedom's song;

Let mortal tongues awake;
Let all that breathe partake;
Let rocks their silence break—
 The song prolong.

4.
Our fathers' God, to thee,
Author of liberty,
 To thee we sing;
Long may our land be bright
With freedom's holy light;
Protect us by thy might,
 Great God, our King.

GOD SAVE THE STATE.

1.
GOD bless our native land!
Firm may she ever stand,
 Through storm and night;
When the wild tempests rave,
Ruler of winds and wave,
Do thou our country save
 By thy great might.

2.
For her our prayer shall rise
To God, above the skies:
 On him we wait;
Thou who art ever nigh,
Guarding with watchful eye,
To thee aloud we cry,
 God save the State!

CONTENTS.

	PAGE		PAGE
A crown of glory bright	104	Come to Jesus, come	5
A Lover of the Lord	138	Come to Jesus, little one	53
Always with us	35	Come to Jesus just now	139
America	140	Come to the fountain	82
Am I a soldier of the cross	129	Come to the manger	74
Around the pure and shining throne	77	Comfort me	80
		Cross and Crown	13
A Starless Crown	33	CHANTS.	
Autumn	105	I was glad when they said unto me	121
Azmon	83		
		Our Father, who art in heaven	91
Bartimeus	121	The Lord is my Shepherd	87
Battling for the Lord	68	The Lord's Prayer	91
Beautiful City	112		
Beautiful Home above	85	Dark is the night	78
Beautiful River	102	Dawn, O golden glory	88
Beautiful Vale of Rest	66	Dear Saviour, all I think or do	55
Beautiful Zion built above	112	Dennis	67
Behold the Lamb of God	28	Do we thirst for living water	81
Bethany	99	Duke Street	119
Blessed Redeemer	11		
Brethren, let us speak for Jesus	65	Easter Anthem	64
Brethren, let us work for Jesus	51	Even me	90
By-and-bye	72		
By faith I view my Saviour bleeding	124	Fade, fade each earthly joy	21
		Father, I stretch my hand to thee	132
Call to the Young	47	Father, whate'er of earthly bliss	83
Cheerfully give	24	Fatherless, motherless, cheerless in grief	60
Children's Praise	113		
Christ the only Refuge	107	Fellow helpers to the truth	15
Christian brethren, one and all	58	Frederick	117
Christ, the Lord, is risen to day	64	From Greenland's icy mountains	130
Climbing up Zion's Hill	56	Fullness in Christ	93
Come, let us learn to sing below	3		
Come, thou fount of every blessing	136	Gallant soldiers, hear the trumpet sounding	6

CONTENTS.

	PAGE
Give, give, cheerfully give	24
Glory in the highest	116
Glorious things of thee are spoken	105
Go and work	78
God bless our native land	140
God bless our school	71
God of my life	83
Going home	138
Grace is free	19
Happy Day	132
Hark! hark! the battle cry	122
Hark! the gentle spirit pleading	5
Heaven is bright	42
Heaven of Rest	13
Heber	91
Here is no rest	101
Here o'er the earth as a stranger	101
Here we throng to praise the Lord	113
Home	116
Home of the blest	59
Homeward bound	128
Hosanna to his name	30
How charming is the place	99
How happy every child of grace	123
How I long to be like Jesus	114
I am waiting by the river	59
I do believe	132
If I come to Jesus	31
I hear my Saviour say	93
I know that heaven is bright	42
I'll sing of Jesus crucified	34
I'll sing with angels	26
I love Jesus	136
I love thy kingdom, Lord	67
I love to think of heaven	134
I'm a pilgrim	136
I'm a soldier, soldier of the cross	32
I'm going to be a soldier	57
I'm kneeling at the door	70
I'm kneeling, Lord, at mercy's gate	70
I'm trying to climb up Zion's hill	56
In that happy land	49
In the Christian's home in glory	110
In the cross of Christ I glory	121
Ives	103

	PAGE
I want to think of Jesus	23
I was glad when they said	121
I would not live alway	117
Jesus came, Jesus came	18
Jesus, I long for thee	125
Jesus is here	84
Jesus is mine	21
Jesus, lover of my soul	107
Jesus loves me	17
Jesus, make me faithful	98
Jesus my all	125
Jesus once lay in a manger	40
Jesus only	18
Jesus paid it all	73
Jesus, tender Saviour	75
Jesus shall reign where'er the sun	119
Jesus, thou art the sinner's friend	133
Jesus will welcome me	96
Jewels	79
Joy among the angels	22
Joyful, joyful now I resign	8
Joyfully, joyfully onward I move	137
Keep on praying	4
Like the heroes who gave us the land	95
Little birds of the forest	46
Little modest violet blue	115
Little Things	115
Long my spirit pined in sorrow	4
Looking unto Jesus	38
Lord, at thy mercy-seat	125
Lord, I hear of showers of blessings	90
Lord, I perish; save, I cried	19
Lord, the way is cold and dreary	9
Love at home	100
Marching on to glory	6
Marching Song	122
Martyn	107
Mary to the Saviour's tomb	107
Mercy's free	124
Merry, merry chiming bells	116
'Mid the pastures green of the blessed isles	89

CONTENTS.

	PAGE		PAGE
Mine the cross and thine the glory	50	Ringing, sweetly ringing	20
		Rock of Ages	128
Missionary Hymn	131		
More like Jesus	37	Sabbath Bells	20
Mount Pisgah	129	Shall I be there	36
Must Jesus bear the cross alone	119	Shall we gather at the river	102
My country, 'tis of thee	140	Shall we know each other there	86
My days are gliding swiftly by	118	Shining Shore	118
My heavenly home is bright and fair	138	Shout the glad tidings	126
		Singing for Jesus	92
My rest is in heaven	52	Slow to anger, full of kindness.	27
My soul with rapture waits for thee	66	Softly on the breath of evening.	63
		Soldiers for Jesus	43
My spirit in hope is rejoicing	96	Soldier of the Cross	32
		Speak, and we will hear	45
Nearer, my God, to thee	99	Speak for Jesus	65
Nearer my home	104	Speak from thy holy word	45
Never give up	43	St. Thomas	99
No sorrow there	134	Sweet Land of Rest	135
Nothing but leaves	41	Sweetly sing	108
Nothing either great or small	73		
		Take thy children home	29
O come to Jesus now	84	Tell me, watchman on the steep	88
O happy day, that fixed my choice	132	The Angel Boatman	10
		The Angel's Welcome	52
O heaven, dear heaven	123	The Banner of Jesus	95
O how my spirit longs for thee.	85	The Bible	44
O land of rest, for thee I sigh	25	The Convert's Song	8
Oh could I with the angels sing	26	The Golden Rule	127
Oh, shall I wear a starless crown	33	The Gospel Ship	106
		The Happy Land	111
Once more, my soul	111	The Happy Long Ago	16
On our way to glory	14	The Invitation	40
One by one we cross the river	10	The Jasper Sea	97
Only just across the river	62	The Lambs of the Upper Fold.	89
Our Father, who art in heaven.	91	The Lord is my Shepherd	87
Our Jesus	46	The Lord's Prayer	91
Out on an ocean all boundless	128	The morning light is breaking	131
Over on the other side	62	The One Petition	83
		The Orphan Wanderer	60
Passing away	109	The Pilgrim's Journey	27
Peterborough	111	The Polar Star	48
Pilgrim, rest awhile	9	The Saviour calls, let every ear	91
Pilgrim, watch and pray	63	The Stone rolled away	12
Press onward	54	The Sweetest Name	114
		There is a happy land	111
Redeeming Love	77	There is beauty all around	100
Remember me	133	There is a name the prophets know	114
Rest for the weary	110		
Return, O wanderer, to thy home	138	There is a realm where Jesus reigns	39

CONTENTS.

Title	Page	Title	Page
There is joy among the angels..	22	We're trav'ling home to heaven above	134
There's a home for us in glory.	72	We're listed in that holy war.	68
They are waiting by the shore.	16	Webb	131
Thine eye can see	55	Welcome Home	39
'Tis the season of Christmas ..	74	We love the Sabbath School	94
To be like Jesus	114	What is it shows my soul the way	44
To-day, if you will hear his voice	109		
To do to others as I would	127	When Christ was journeying here below	30
Trav'lers in a desert land	14		
Up and doing	51	When he cometh	79
Up for thy life, young soul	47	When saints gather round thee.	36
		When the morning light	69
Waiting by the River	7	When torn is the bosom	116
Watching, hoping, praying	81	When we hear the music ringing	86
We are a group of happy children	94	When we've crossed the Jasper sea	97
We are trav'ling home to heaven	49		
We are waiting by the river	9	While walking the vale	13
Weak and sinful, O my Father	80	Who are these in bright array..	113
We'll wait till Jesus comes	25	Who is he in yonder stall	76
Weary not, my brother	38	Will you go	134
Weary wand'rer o'er the main	48	Why do we linger	29
We're happy, dear Saviour	12	Work, for the night is coming..	120

www.ingramcontent.com/pod-product-compliance
Lightning Source LLC
Chambersburg PA
CBHW022131160426
43197CB00009B/1232